MW01295704

# The Wisdom Walk
## To Self-Mastery

Ancient Wisdom *for* Transforming Pain

Jojopahmaria Nsoroma

**BALBOA.**
PRESS

A DIVISION OF HAY HOUSE

Copyright © 2019 Jojopahmaria Nsoroma.

All rights reserved. No part of this book may be used or reproduced by
any means, graphic, electronic, or mechanical, including photocopying,
recording, taping or by any information storage retrieval system
without the written permission of the author except in the case of
brief quotations embodied in critical articles and reviews.

Scripture quotations marked KJV are from the Holy Bible, King James
Version (Authorized Version). First published in 1611. Quoted from the KJV
Classic Reference Bible, Copyright © 1983 by The Zondervan Corporation.

Balboa Press books may be ordered through booksellers or by contacting:

Balboa Press
A Division of Hay House
1663 Liberty Drive
Bloomington, IN 47403
www.balboapress.com
1 (877) 407-4847

Because of the dynamic nature of the Internet, any web addresses or
links contained in this book may have changed since publication and
may no longer be valid. The views expressed in this work are solely those
of the author and do not necessarily reflect the views of the publisher,
and the publisher hereby disclaims any responsibility for them.

The author of this book does not dispense medical advice or prescribe the use
of any technique as a form of treatment for physical, emotional, or medical
problems without the advice of a physician, either directly or indirectly. The
intent of the author is only to offer information of a general nature to help
you in your quest for emotional and spiritual well-being. In the event you use
any of the information in this book for yourself, which is your constitutional
right, the author and the publisher assume no responsibility for your actions.

Cover art and design by award-winning impressionist and
plein air artist, Shelby Keefe, www.studioshelby.com.

Print information available on the last page.

ISBN: 978-1-9822-2658-9 (sc)
ISBN: 978-1-9822-2659-6 (e)

Balboa Press rev. date: 05/09/2019

# CONTENTS

## PART 4 THE WISDOM WALK HEALING JOURNEY

## PART 5 WISDOM WALKING AT THE MOVIES

# Dedication Page

*I* dedicate this book and the healing energy that it contains to all of the emotionally courageous men of the Wisdom Walk to Self-Mastery Program – past, present, and future. It is an honor to have been called to serve you.

# Epigraph

*Thus, one can say to a healer, "Teach me what you know"; but the better request to make of the healer is, "Teach me about what teaches you." Since the source, and home, of indigenous technology is nature and the world of Spirit, to that source you must go in order to learn and grow and evolve.*

—Dr. Malidoma Patrice Somé, Ph.D., *The Healing Wisdom of Africa*, p.81

# Invocation

*Ancestors, Ancestors, Ancestors!*
*Thank you for hearing my call.*
*Thank you for your dreams of a better time,*
*Of a better life, of a better world.*
*You are my closest Allies and great Emissaries between my Self and Creator,*
*So, I call upon you now to guide my every thought, every word, every sentence,*
*Every paragraph, every chapter of this book, for truly, I cannot do this work alone.*
*I need your help, your guidance, your wisdom, and your love,*
*That I may stay true to my highest purpose, and keep my promise to those*
*For whom this work is intended.*
*Pass my prayer for a good work, a right work, on to Creator,*
*And I say Thank you, Thank you, Thank you,*
*to Creator and you for all of what you do for me*
*In ways known and unknown.*
*May this be so, May this be so, and May this be so.*
*Ashé!*

# PREFACE AND INTRODUCTION

*O*nce upon a time, I was standing in my kitchen at my urban shaman hut, 4137A North 41st Street, when my cell phone rang. It was in June of 2008, and I'd only been living in my own apartment again for 9 months, after being on a 6 ½ year nomadic adventure around the country where I relied upon the kindness and generosity of friends, family, colleagues and even strangers. Those 6 ½ years were the result of my commitment to learning how to fully surrender to my calling as a wisdom keeper of ancient indigenous teachings and techniques for transforming pain into joy and love. I'll save the details of my epic journey for another book, but I can tell you, that by the time I was standing in that kitchen, answering my cell phone, I had achieved my goal.

The phone call that I received happened on what was a gorgeous spring afternoon, and the call was truly and literally a spiritual call. When I said "hello" no one answered, but my phone captured the name of the caller, and I could hear muted voices talking in the background. I called out my friend's name "Shawn" three times before accepting that she couldn't hear me and had not intentionally dialed my number. So, I hung up (Oops! *old skool* terminology for I hit the "end" button), and then called back to let her know that her phone was dialing me. When she answered my call, her first words to me were, "Jojopah! I was just talking about you! I'm having lunch with the executive director of the Alma Center, Terri Strodthoff, and she's looking for a healer!"

As a result of that phone call, I was able to experience one of my dreams come true. I was able to successfully establish a human services program that integrated African spirituality, science, and storytelling for the purpose of transforming emotional pain. I call this program, *Wisdom Walk to Self-Mastery*. For five years I provided a twelve-week, thrice a week, two hours per session, intensive healing process for men. My participants were referred through domestic violence court. All of these men had severe adverse childhood experiences, which included repeated physical, emotional and sexual abuse. Many of them in childhood and/or adolescence, had someone they knew and loved shot and killed. Sometimes, it happened right in front of them.

Most of the men referred to my program had been cycling through the criminal justice system from about ages 13 through 35. My program was often a last resort before imprisonment became the only way they could survive in the world. Their lives were a revolving door from being on the streets to being in a jail cell, with uncontrolled criminal and violent behavior defining who they believed themselves to be. So how in the world, you may ask, was I able to effectively teach the majority of these men to take charge of their lives, control their dysregulated behaviors, and choose to make loving contributions to each other, their families and communities? The answer is found between the covers of this book.

Initially, this book was designed to be a resource for all the graduates of the program. I always let them know that the 12-week program was just the opening to their life-long journey to heal from their traumas and become the best version of themselves. It made sense to put into writing the wisdom I had shared so that they could get easy access to reminders and validation. During the time that I first began drafting a book outline, I had the opportunity to use some of the *Wisdom Walk* methodology with a group of professional women. The process was very effective in helping them uncover and shift old belief systems that were blocking their experiences of fulfillment, both personally and professionally. From working with these women, I learned that the methodology of the *Wisdom Walk* program could work with anyone who wanted to eliminate childhood pain, struggling and suffering, and 'unhappy endings' from their adult life. It is now my great pleasure to make this information more accessible to all those who need its medicine.

The primary intent of this book is to grow your consciousness. I want you and every human being on this planet to believe and learn that emotional pain can be transformed rather than transferred. I also want you to believe that you can learn to avoid feeling victimized by others and life itself. This book will take you on a virtual journey through your inner landscape— that invisible and most powerful part of who you are. Like any landscape, it has hills, mountains, valleys, forests, lakes and shores. What makes your inner landscape different from an external one, is that you can choose to change the unwanted parts without having to use a back hoe or dynamite! Your inner landscape is the land of raw emotions, feelings, memories, fears, dreams, anger, passion, hidden desires, childhood conditioning, and core beliefs. It is also the land of hidden and deeply rooted pain that you may yet have to discover.

The number '5' is very important to me, as you will discover, so the book is divided into five parts. Parts One and Two will provide the basic information and vocabulary to support your virtual journey through your inner landscape. In Parts Three and Four you will learn how the *Wisdom Walk* technology can be effectively utilized, as well as how to apply it to situations that are emotionally painful and challenging. Last but not least, Part Five will take you to the movies that I use to help illustrate more clearly the wisdom of *Wisdom Walk*.

To sum it all up, this book is designed to enable you to uncover, accept, transform and heal emotional pain. Traumatic experiences teach fear. The *Wisdom Walk to Self-Mastery* teaches love. The information I share in this book can transport you away from the belief that the world is out to 'get' you, and into the truth that the world is out to 'gift' you.

Before discovering the teachings and methodologies

contained in this book, I was living with chronic depression and constant fear, even though there was no immediate reason for it. I never believed I could have a lifestyle that wasn't always about struggling, suffering, pain, and despair. My best efforts to be and remain successful and financially fit always got railroaded by someone or something over which I had no control. I believed in God but couldn't believe that I was deserving of my fulfillment in life. I often questioned whether my life was worth living.

That all changed when I chose to leave the pavement of life as I knew it and stepped out onto a path of the *unknown*. I call this unique path my wisdom walk. It took me to new and unchartered places within my inner landscape. It also took me out of my familiar external landscape as I physically traveled around the country learning about my hidden pain, how it was ruling my life, and how I could change for the better. In the process, I also discovered my hidden strengths, deepened my connection to my Greater Order and Direction, and realized the truth about my earthly existence.

You do not have to physically travel, as I did, to reap the benefits of this process. You can remain in the same environment, the same job, and the same intimate relationship. In fact, what you know becomes essential to learning what you don't know. The really good news is that once you've made the commitment to walk the path of change, healing, growth, and evolution, you can't fail. You will reach the 'Land of Fulfillment', the place where "happy endings" are yours and free for the taking.

Now, let me be very clear about the fact that having fulfillment in life doesn't mean that nothing bad ever happens. Oh, no! Challenges, troubles, and disappointments will always occur. But, once you have learned to *wisdom walk*, you no longer take any of it personally. You no longer believe that bad things happen because you are bad. You are able to understand and believe that your blessings can show up in many different ways and take many different forms. *There is much treasure in trouble.* As I said before, wisdom walking enables you to live the belief that the world is out to gift you --not get you!

On a final note, I want you to know that what I'm talking about in this book is truly a wisdom walk — not a wisdom run or a wisdom sprint! Journeying through your internal landscape takes time, patience, and faith. You have to respect the journey more than hurrying to the destination. So, if you are ready to find out what this is all about, and begin your *wisdom walk,* just turn the page. May your journey to your inner landscape be a very rich and rewarding experience. May you discover more about the truth of who you really are. May you believe at the end of this book that it is never too late for your "happy endings" in life. And so it is! Ashe!

*Jojopahmaria Nsoroma*
*Milwaukee, Wisconsin*
*July 4th, 2015*

# Part One

## EVERYONE CAN LEARN TO HEAL

# Chapter 1

# Any Pain Not Transformed, Will Be Transferred

## The Message of Pigpen

One of the most popular and influential newspaper comic strips of all time is called, Peanuts. For 50 years, its illustrator and author, Charles M. Schultz, used the daily antics of a group of children and an introspective dog, to raise consciousness about human behavior and make fun of current events. Although the lead characters — Charlie Brown, Snoopy, Lucy, and Linus, were very captivating, as a child I was always fascinated by "Pigpen." Here was this little kid walking within his own private dirt and dust storm, looking dignified and ignoring the negative reactions to his appearance. On the Peanuts official website, I found this quote by Charles Schultz:

> "Pigpen is a human soil bank who raises a cloud of dust on a perfectly clean street and passes out gum drops that are invariably black."

Now that I'm more grown up and conscious-minded, Pigpen for me is a perfect illustration of what it physically must look like when we are unconsciously transferring our emotional pain out into the world. We just go about our business, too emotionally shut down to care or be aware of what we are silently and invisibly doing. It is awfully painful to know that we can be so ignorant of what we are creating for ourselves and others when we are transferring our pain.

According to indigenous shamans and modern scientists, human beings are essentially energetic beings. This basically means that we have the ability to give and receive energies in a non-physical manner. Emotional pain seems to be one of those energies that we humans know how to share very easily and effortlessly. Most of the time, we are oblivious to how and even why we are doing it. Now, the idea that emotional pain can be transferred from one person to another, or even to groups of people, is really nothing new. In fact, this phenomenon was so well understood and believed by our tribal ancestors, that they regularly performed rituals and ceremonies to make sure that one person's pain did not affect the health and harmony of the entire tribe. Over the centuries, particularly in Western civilization, the pursuit of wealth, comfort and external power has left little time for remembering and practicing the communal transformation of emotional pain.

My parents were born before World War II in the Jim Crow South of the United States. A popular saying when they were growing up was, "children are to be seen and not heard," so they became what is known as The Silent Greatest Generation. The culture they awoke to was framed by the Great Depression, an unprecedented global war, and racial oppression. It is clearly understandable why their emotions took a back seat to daily survival. Both of my parents, along with the majority of their generation, found it extremely challenging to discuss, let alone process, their emotional pain. It wasn't until the 1960s, the time of groundbreaking civil rights, slogans of "peace not war", and the commitment to let it all hang out, that slowly and steadily emotional pain became a topic for open discussion.

There were no "Self-Help" sections in the libraries or bookstores back then. Fortunately for us today, self-help books, CDs, and videos are an essential part of our New Age culture for emotional intelligence, wellness, and human potential. We do not have to walk around like Pigpen, unconsciously handing out black gum drops. We can uncover and transform pain from our past --and that of our ancestors too.

## The Pain Body Decoded

When you've experienced something painful, that you didn't have the time or support to openly and freely express your feelings about, that pain will remain with you until you consciously and correctly release it. Eckhart Tolle, a noted author and teacher of conscious human evolution, calls our trapped pain our pain body. Just like our physical bodies, pain bodies come in all shapes and sizes. Everyone's pain body is unique to their own experiences of pain, in all its various forms --physical, emotional, mental, and spiritual. The one thing all pain bodies have in common is their unrelenting hunger for more pain. Our pain body will invisibly and silently attract painful people, places, and situations into our lives in order to get fed. It feeds on all types of drama and any situation or experience where we feel victimized, abused, betrayed, disrespected, neglected, ignored, abandoned, disappointed, unappreciated, or of where we have been taken advantage.

The more the pain body is allowed to lord over our lives and attempt to satisfy its insatiable hunger, the harder and more disheartening it becomes to like and love ourselves. No matter how dignified and together we may appear on the outside, on the inside we will be a mess. It is also important to know that any attempt to sedate or ignore our emotional pain is futile. All forms of addictive behaviors --drugs, alcohol, indiscriminate sex, gambling, shopping, eating, etc., are evidence of a very active and hungry pain body.

When we are seemingly caught in a never-ending cycle of unhappy and unfulfilling experiences, we automatically take on the conscious belief system of victim, or victim consciousness, which can sound like the following:

"my best efforts always get thwarted"

"things never work out for me like they do for other people"

"I'll never have a happy ending where relationships are concerned"

"I'm always so nice to people but they're always mean to me"

and my personal favorite, "the world is out to get me!"

I have to tell you that these belief systems are sinful. I'm using that term very purposely because the truth of who you are, as a human being with a never-ending, lifetime membership to Eternity, is just the opposite of those beliefs. Your best efforts will always meet with some form of opposition, including self-sabotage, but that can be overcome. Things will only work out when the time is right. You have to have a 'happy ending' in your relationship with your Self before you can experience that with anyone else. Just because someone is mean to you doesn't mean you failed at being nice and kind. Being nice and kind must never be dependent upon how someone else is or is not able to receive it. Most importantly, the world is out to "gift" you. Everything that happens to you is designed to heal and grow you into the very best version of your Self. There is great treasure in every bit of trouble or tragedy — if you are willing to find it.

Believing and living from the above truths is not an easy or overnight process. It takes time, commitment, discipline, faith, and patient endurance. It also takes becoming absolutely conscious of the embedded pain you are still carrying from the past and how you are unconsciously transferring it onto others, as well as yourself.

Here are some of the most common ways in which we transfer our emotional pain:

- any form of aggression or abuse –physical, sexual, mental, emotional or spiritual
- domestic violence, whether physical, verbal (making threats), or psychological (being domineering and oppressive or manipulative)
- using control dramas: passive or aggressive attempts to control people and situations in order to feel mentally safe; including playing "poor me", acting aloof, and being intimidating or interrogating
- being judgmental and critical
- being unjustly accusatory and blaming
- being jealous and envious of others
- teasing, putting down, or shaming others
- gossiping
- taking things personally and being on the defensive

From this list we can see that emotional pain can be transferred physically as well as non-physically. We can also see how many of these we do on a daily basis and consider them as just a normal part of interpersonal relationships. Hopefully this list gives you pause to realize how much, and how often, you are unconsciously transferring versus transforming your embedded emotional pain.

Most of us know that if we are in a relationship where violence is occurring, regardless of the frequency, that behavior is considered a crime. But if you are in a relationship where you and your partner are having a regular nonphysical pain body "slugfest", please know that this behavior can easily lead to the physical violence.

The great news is that you can interrupt the pain body from ruining your life. The first step is to know that you have one and get acquainted with it. Make a commitment to yourself to learn what it looks like, sounds like, feels like, tastes and smells like when your pain body is active and hungry. You can't shift out of being a victim to your pain if you aren't aware of it. This is called becoming consciously aware. Later in this book I will share some tools and resources that you can use to take back your control of yourself and put your pain body in its proper place.

## My Pain Body Story

My pain body primarily showed up as a huge control drama. I'd wake up in the morning just to be able to control everyone and everything around me. It wasn't until I read The Celestine Prophecy, by James Redfield, that I found a vocabulary for how I was driving myself, and everyone around me, crazy. Recently I found on that author's website, celestinevision.com, more details about the four most common ways in which control drama shows up. First, there's the "poor me" approach where you manipulate attention by getting people to feel sorry for you. Second, there's playing "aloof", a form of passive aggression where being silent and detached draws people's attention to you to find out what is the matter. Third is the "intimidator." This is where you invalidate people through judgement, criticism, and being a 'know-it- all'. Through your intimidation, you are indicating that who they are and what they believe is just not enough.

The fourth most common control drama is that of the "interrogator." This is where you act as judge and jury regarding what someone did or didn't do by playing "20 questions". In this manner you are hoping to expose the fact that they are wrong, and you are right. The true irony or joke here is that all of this control drama behavior is driven by a very deep and unconscious fear of the 'Boogey Man or Woman'. In other words, you believe that everyone is always out to get you, and so you'd better find a way to control them before that happens.

By the time I began my life as a career woman, many years ago, I had mastered all forms of control drama. On top of that,

I was totally a Pigpen. I physically appeared very dignified and together in my Evan Picone silk suits and Italian leather shoes, flashing the latest Anne Klein jewelry, and a $250-head of the finest African braiding by one of the most talented hairdressers in Harlem. I was a powerful *Afra-American Buppy* (slang for *Female Black Urban Professional*).

At one point in my career, I was traveling around the country as an administrator for a national human services organization, totally convinced that I was the nicest, kindness, and most considerate human being on the planet. Then one day, my staff of three people sat me down and told me about my control drama. They found me intimidating and untrusting of their ability to support my efforts. Of course I went immediately into denial, felt victimized by what they said. I believed they were jealous of me and trying to thwart my efforts. I felt angry and betrayed. I couldn't feel their pain because I was working hard not to feel my own. I resigned from my position a short time afterwards.

At that time in my life, I had no idea that I was repressing the memories of early childhood sexual abuse. My mind had sheltered me from them and kept them deeply buried in my subconscious, along with the full physical and emotional impact of what had happened to me. I was between the ages of two and four when the repeated transfer of pain occurred. At that age, I had no language or vocabulary for what was happening to me. I was forty years old when I finally had recall, and it was then that I began my life-long journey for healing and emotional growth.

I first become acquainted with my pain body during my initial healing process in which I utilized psychotherapy, and an anti-depression medication to keep me from harming myself. It was also during this initial process that I learned how any pain that is not transformed will be transferred. I discovered how negative self-talk, and self-sabotage were my constant companions. I learned how deeply resentful I was of men and realized why none of my intimate relationships were fulfilling. I learned that despite my designer clothes and professional mannerisms, I knew nothing about self-love.

Today I still have a pain body, but what started out as Godzilla has been shrunk down to the small, lavender colored, stuffed toy dragon. I keep her on top of my bureau as a visual reminder. I'm reminding myself that my pain body will exist as long as I am alive and kicking, but now I get to be in charge. My pain body can only take me to painful people and places if I allow it.

Over the years I've learned to recognize and avoid the people, places and situations that will trigger the emergence of my core pain. When I've been blindsided and find myself in a situation that doesn't feel good or support the truth of who I am, I get out as quickly as possible. I've also learned how to take on full responsibility for recognizing my pain, versus taking on someone else's. I am now able to transform my pain by using the ancient wisdom I will share with you in this book.

The phrase, "any pain not transformed, will be transferred" is what I call my ministry. I got this phrase from my dear friend and mentor, William Graustein. He told me he got it from a friend, and now I'm passing it on to you. It is one of the initial teachings I shared with the men in the *Wisdom Walk to Self-Mastery* program. I told them if they heard or learned nothing else during our time together, they would still graduate. Being willing to take responsibility for not dumping your pain onto others, despite how they may have dumped theirs onto you, is a very noble thing to do.

In the next chapter, I will discuss how pain can become a way to know yourself, why that doesn't work, and what you can do to change or avoid that belief.

For more information on:

**Pain Body:** Chapters 5 & 6 of Eckhart Tolle's, *A New Earth*: awakening to your life's purpose

**Control Dramas:** https://www.celestinevision.com/control-dramas/

**Pigpen:** http://www.peanuts.com/characters/pigpen/#.VZwsV_m0qSo

# Chapter 2

# You Are Not Your Pain

## Pain Cannot Tell You Who You Are

O ne of my most favorite lines from the first *Matrix* film occurs when Neo is being taken to see the Oracle for the first time. He's riding in the back of the black 1965 Lincoln Continental, looking out the window at places he used to believe were real. He kind of shakes his head and ask Trinity, who is sitting beside him, "What does it all mean?". She replies, *"That the Matrix cannot tell you who you are."*

Emotional pain is very much like the Matrix. If you haven't ever seen this film, what I'm talking about is a form of virtual reality where you are not physically experiencing events, but your mind engages with the illusions enough that you do experience physical sensations. Emotional pain that is not consciously released within a short period after you first experience it, can turn into your own personal Matrix.

As I talked about in the first chapter, embedded emotional pain can become a pain body, and take over management of the real you. It can convince you that you are not worthy of love, that there is something wrong with you, that you are supposed to be unhappy, that you are a victim, and that you will never know fulfillment in life. Just like Neo, the lead character who literally has to wake up to the truth of who he is really, we too have to wake up from all of the false beliefs that emotional pain has brought to us. Emotional pain is not the truth of who you are. It can just feel that way.

Here is a quick test to determine whether or not emotional pain has created a personal Matrix for you. Go look into a mirror. Stare at yourself for 3 minutes and notice what chatter about yourself comes into your mind. If the chatter is unconditional love, then you are in charge of your pain body. But if the chatter is negative and invalidating, full of put downs, then your emotional pain has created a Matrix, and your pain body is keeping you from the truth of who you are.

Identifying with pain begins in childhood. This is why it is such an easy, effortless, and unconscious thing to do. Modern science has produced evidence that children do not have access to abstract thinking. What this means in plain language is that children cannot internally ask, or process, the deeper questions about why something bad happened to them. The only thing they are capable of doing is to blame themselves. In other words, they believe that bad things happen to them because they are bad. As a result, childhood pain can become a life-long lens through which someone sees and understands themselves, and the world around them.

The story of Ebenezer Scrooge in the classic Christmas tale by Charles Dickens, *A Christmas Carol*, is a great example of this. Scrooge is the meanest man in town, and on top of that, he's extremely stingy and insensitive. He's what today we would call *emotionally retarded*. This soul-less and heartless man is given the opportunity for redemption by being taken back to review his childhood. It is here that we learn the reason he has no love in his life. He was horribly neglected by his father and family, even at Christmas time. Through Divine intervention, Scrooge is able to transcend his past pain, and become the best version of himself. The ultimate message of this story is that Scrooge was not his pain. He just didn't know that he wasn't.

# Pain as a Cosmic Messenger

Emotional pain has a purpose, and that purpose isn't about making you miserable or separating you from the truth of who you are. Every person on this planet has experienced emotional pain which is rooted in a childhood core wound. Even His Holiness, the Dalai Lama! At age 5, he was enthroned as the supreme spiritual leader for Tibet and separated from his parents and family. Although he was given tons of attention and support from other adults, not being with his own family in his family home had to be painful. Here is a list of common core wounds that can occur during childhood:

- Abandonment and/or Separation from family (Physical and Emotional); Includes death or illness of parents or their unavailability because of divorce, active military service, addiction to drugs or alcohol, etc.
- Betrayal (Trust is established then betrayed.) Includes ambivalence or emotional instability of caretakers including the mental or physical illness of parents
- Abuse (physical, emotional, sexual, ritual); includes lack of appropriate boundaries or inappropriate behavior by parents, siblings or other family members
- Stolen childhood/Caretaking of parents or siblings; being forced to take on adult responsibilities before we are ready
- Lack of Limits, Low Expectations, Overprotection, or Too much freedom
- Guilt, False Responsibility (for a parent or sibling's death or illness, etc.)
- Birth Trauma, Birth Defects, Premature Birth
- Serious or Extensive Illness in Childhood
- Not being wanted, Unplanned pregnancy

- Rejection and/or Neglect by a Parent; Post-partum depression of mother
- Persecution/Bullying by Siblings or other children, as well as repeated humiliation, criticism, shaming, blaming by parents, caretakers, or significant others

(The above information was excerpted and edited from **Embracing Our True Self**: *A New Paradigm Approach to Healing Our Wounds, Finding Our Gifts, and Fulfilling our Spiritual Purpose*, by **Paul Ferrini**, pp.35-37.)

Clearly, experiencing emotional pain is the 3rd thing you can count on in life besides death and taxes. It would then make sense that our pain is not our ultimate destination, but just an inseparable and required part of our journey to living authentically, joyously, and with purpose.

Emotional pain in adulthood is a powerful cosmic messenger, and we seem to know this naturally. Have you ever noticed that when something really painful shows up, usually the first words out of our mouths is "Oh God!" Deep inside we understand that when pain shows up, something bigger than our intellect or ego is at work. This is simply because the pain is nothing we would choose for ourselves. There has to be some bigger meaning behind it, or at least we hope so!

Believing that you pain is a messenger is the first step in the pain transformation process. When you choose to consider the messenger role of pain in your adult life, you will realize that it wasn't designed to stay with you for your entire life. Messengers are supposed to come and go. But in our modern culture, there is so much support for holding onto emotional pain that it easy to forget that we can choose to transform it.

We talk about anger management rather than pain elimination. We fall into martyrdom and wear our heartbreaks and betrayals like medals of honor. Modern culture also provides a great variety of ways to ignore and sedate our pain.

There are gambling casinos, "gentleman" clubs, mega shopping stores and malls, "all-you-can-eat" restaurants, and easy access to illegal and pharmaceutical drugs — to name just a few. You just have to wonder where the United States and increasingly global economy would be without all of the stuck emotional pain that is being carried around. Hmm!

So if pain is a messenger, what is the message? Well, the cosmic message of pain is the same for everyone, although the details of the message will be unique to each individual. *The universal cosmic message of emotional pain is that there is something in your past that needs to be healed.* It's that basic, that simple, and that challenging. Because our child brains were not able to process painful events beyond blaming ourselves, by the time we reach adulthood we have lots of buried shame, guilt, and self-hatred. Despite these emotional road blocks, our adult emotional pain can be the "open sesame" cry to reveal the hidden, unhealed wounds of our past; and also that of our ancestors.

## *Pain as a Great Teacher*

All messengers are supposed to help us learn something we didn't know about before, and pain is no different. In fact, I truly consider pain to be the greatest of all teachers. So what, you may be asking, does pain teach us? Well, that depends on how you choose to learn. The choice you have is simple. You can either learn from pain through love, or through fear.

Learning through fear means emotional pain will make you right about being a victim to life. You will be emotionally triggered back to the age you were in childhood when you experienced your first great disappointment or mistreatment. You pain body will be allowed to run your show again. You'll blame others for your pain, and not consider the negative contributions of your own pain body. Or, you'll embrace co-dependency more deeply, blame yourself entirely, and then punish yourself by behaving in unhealthy and unloving ways. Learning from pain through fear will have you believing in the lie that the world is out to get you.

When you choose to learn the teachings of your emotional pain through love, then the experience is just the opposite. Instead of claiming victimhood, you embrace self-compassion, and accept the fact that pain is a necessary part of the healing process. You are able to remind yourself that healing doesn't feel good, but the results make confronting your pain well worth it. You also stop blaming anyone for your pain through the practice forgiveness. You are able to take on full responsibility for your feelings, which leads to acceptance and gratitude for your pain. Then, you are able to ask the pain to help you discover the root of your suffering, so you can be free to live your truth. Learning from pain through love will validate, and have you live the cosmic truth that the world is out to "gift" you.

Choosing to learn from pain in a self-loving manner takes a huge commitment on the healing journey. It's one of those things that doesn't happen overnight. In my experience, you usually have to first choose pain as the false-fear-teacher over and over and over again, until you just finally get sick and tired of all the negative feelings and energy. When you finally hit bottom with anything, it creates a desire and willingness to rise to the top. You find yourself wanting to open your mind, heart and soul to the questioning of your victimhood. Thoughts will emerge in your brain like:

> *What if this pain is making me more compassionate with myself and others?*
> *What if this pain is a pass key to being more wise and able to see the truth in people and situations?*
> *What if this pain is teaching me that I've got lots of work to do with myself before I can experience fulfillment in life?*

Yes, it's important to know, that once you allow yourself to experience pain as a loving teacher — who only wants you to win, then you begin to find it harder to treat it like your tormentor and executioner. This doesn't mean we have to like emotional pain. That's way crazy! It just means that we have to learn to appreciate it because it is a cosmic messenger, and ultimately a great teacher.

## My Pain Identification Story

My core wound is about being burdensome to my mother. I call this my *momma drama*. She became a single-mother during her pregnancy with me, and already had two other small children. The separation between her and my father was full of shame and embarrassment for her. He was exposed as a polygamist, had four other wives, and had impregnated an older teenage girl at the same time my mother was pregnant with me. All of her feelings of anger, rage, grief, sorrow, and shame were transferred to me as I was developing in her womb. I can't imagine what my mother went through, enduring such deep heartbreak. She always told me, my sister, and brother that she loved my father. I have such compassion for her and marvel at the amount of courage she had to muster up in order to give birth to me, for which I of course I'm truly thankful. But, my core wound was rooted in her pain, and for over 35 years I believed I was her mistake. I believed I was her burden, and unconsciously I believed I didn't deserve my 'happy endings' in life.

My identifying with the pain of my core wound powerfully emerged during the summer I went to a YMCA day camp. It was all about hair! I was 12 years old, and about to enter junior high school, the 7th grade. At the camp, there was swimming every day. I loved being in the water but had no idea how much the chlorine was damaging my hair.

I'd always had an uneasy relationship with my hair. I was born bald, and my hair was never as thick or as long as my older sister's. Quite naturally, my mother projected her ideas of feminine beauty onto me, so I always had to have bangs because I had what was called "a high forehead." This meant that my hair line wasn't pretty enough.

I hated having to get my hair pressed with a hot comb and curling irons every two weeks and wearing those pink foam rollers to bed every night with a head rag. Nappy edges and nappy hair was, and unfortunately for many still is, ugly and unacceptable. So, when the chlorine dried out the shafts of my thin and fragile hair, my hair broke off so much that my mom said I looked like "a picked chicken!"

Afros weren't in style enough yet, so my mom continued to press my hair, feeling utterly frustrated that there wasn't enough for her to work with. She could hardly get any hair around those painful rollers at night. Doing my hair was burdensome to her because she couldn't style it the way she wanted. I blamed myself for going swimming too much, and for not having hair as "good" as her or my sister. I began to believe I was ugly.

This belief really got cemented the following summer when she took me, and my brother and sister, on vacation to California. She bought me a wig to wear, because she didn't want to have to be bothered with my hair. I hated that wig. I hated myself.

My ugly belief system became my 'best friend' all through my teenage years, and even into young adulthood. I may have been an "A" student and graduated from Fordham University *magna cum laude* (with high honors), but having short, un-stylable hair made me an ugly duckling girl. It was until I was 24 years old that I began to think I might be beautiful.

By the summer of 1981, African hair-braiding had come into style. My sister gave me my first hair extensions, with silver beads on the ends. For the first time since the YMCA wreaked havoc on my hair, I looked into the mirror and liked what I saw. Braids became my new 'best friend' and my saviour. Braids freed me up from hot combs, rollers, head rags, and the fear of my hair getting nappy if I got caught in the rain. I quickly found a professional hair dresser in Harlem, Riqui Braithwaite, who with her skill and artistry turned me into an African Queen.

For the next 24 years I made human hair extensions responsible for my beauty. I had a brief time wearing dread locks, and also worshipped them as the cause for my beauty. It wasn't until I turned 51 years old that I was able to let go of my attachment to hair as being responsible for whether or not I was beautiful. I had received a clear message from Spirit that I needed to cut my dread locks, but I was scared to death. How could I be beautiful, and how could people like me, if I didn't have hair? Then, I reconnected with someone from my past who I loved dearly but who was stuck in the past. This person was holding onto an old belief and old pain, and it was keeping them in a very guarded misery. When I realized that this person was mirroring me, and that I too was holding on to old, old stuff in my life, I cut off my dreads and had my head shaved bare; just like when I was born.

As a result of that action, I was reborn into my natural and authentic beauty. I looked in the mirror and saw my essence smiling back at me --high forehead and all! I realized for the first time that it wasn't my hair that made me beautiful. My beauty came from the inside out, and it was my choice. As India Arie sings, *"I am not my hair!"* Since that experience, I have forgiven my mom and all of my ancestors who never learned to love themselves unconditionally. In addition, I have also forgiven myself for spending 39 years of my life believing that I wasn't beautiful—unless I had a good head of hair.

# Chapter 3

# Happy Endings are Your Destiny

## Life is Meant for Happy Endings

The phrase, *having your happy endings in life,* is my way of saying *being fulfilled in life.* Fulfillment shows up in your life when you consciously choose to live through your higher purpose, which always involves making significant and loving contributions to the well-being of others. Fulfillment is an experience that everybody needs to have in order to appreciate all the trials and tribulations of being human. We don't go through challenges and hardships just to be going through them. Every struggle in your life is designed to grow you for a life of joy, happiness and fulfillment. It's hard to believe in happy endings when you are going through difficulties, but when you come through difficulties you have the choice to be wiser, more compassionate, strengthened in your ability to persevere, and closer to your Greater Order & Direction.

To achieve fulfillment in life, you have to first believe in it and choose to commit yourself to learning how to have it. A life without fulfillment is a life of quiet desperation, chronic depression, bitterness, and negativity. Remember Ebenezer Scrooge, the main character of Charles Dickens's *A Christmas Carol,* before his redemption? He was so negative about life and people because of his childhood wounds. He shut down his emotions and gave up the love of his life for the empty and unfulfilling pursuit of money. Being wealthy can't make you happy or fulfilled. Unless you have a loving purpose in life and know that happiness has to come from inside of you, no amount of money will ever be enough.

I wholeheartedly believe that "happy endings" aren't supposed to only happen in fairytales or 'rom coms'—romantic comedy films. Every time we make a heartfelt wish, or dream an authentic dream, or hear a sacred calling, we are destined to experience joy, peace and fulfillment. You'll notice that I specified the type of wish, dream and calling. I did that purposely because only what is in alignment, in synch, with your unique purpose in life can manifest. Dreams that don't come true are either not for you or will manifest way different from what you imagined.

Wishes, dreams and callings that are truly yours are the ones that pursue you, even as you pursue them. There will be many moments of synchronicity and things falling effortlessly into place. You can tell when your desire or calling is authentic because it will be persistent, it won't go away over time because it comes from a Greater Order and Direction —not your ego. You don't feel right if you aren't participating in their manifestation process. It is for this reason that the fulfillment of your dreams, or having your happy endings, is an essential part of life. Life is meant for happy endings.

As I said before, if you want to have happy endings in life, you must first believe in them. This is not an easy thing to do, especially if your pain body is in charge of your life. Making anyone or anything, besides you and your God, responsible for your happy endings can also be a huge barrier along your journey to fulfillment. Unconsciously remaining loyal to the suffering of your Ancestors will also create much self-sabotage, as you attempt to pursue your wishes, dreams and callings. The good news is that despite any and all barriers in your mind, you can still choose to learn how to have fulfillment. You can choose to believe you deserve happy endings in life, you can have faith in your dreams, and you can practice the required amount of patience to allow them to manifest.

# A Journey of Belief, Faith, and Patience

One of my favorite stories that beautifully validates what I'm talking about is the story of Michaela DePrince. Michaela is currently 20 years old and a professional classical ballet dancer. Her life began very tragically. She was born in Sierra Leone, a West African country, during the time that it was being ravaged by a horrific civil war. At age 3 she was orphaned. Her beloved father was shot and killed by rebels, and her mother died of starvation shortly after. Michaela, whose birth name is Mabinty Bangura, was taken to an orphanage where she suffered from malnourishment and mistreatment. She has a skin condition called *vitiligo*, which causes white freckles on her face and neck. A head staff person labelled her "a devil's child." Children in the orphanage were given a number that ranked their level of potential for being adopted. Michaela was given the lowest number.

As fate would have it, the orphanage was bombed, and Michaela along with other survivors fled to a refugee camp. It was here that she, at age 3, got hold of a magazine picture that the wind blew up against the fence in the yard in which she played. The picture was of a beautiful ballerina wearing a white tutu and a lovely smile. Michaela had never seen anything like that before, and she had no language for what she was looking at. All she knew, is that she wanted to be that when she grew up.

*"I was in such a bad situation, so the fact that this person was so happy and enjoying life — it made me hope that I could be that happy someday."*

(above quote from interview in TeenVogue magazine, July 20, 2012: *Defying Gravity: Teen Ballerina Michaela DePrince* by Giannella Garrett)

By age 4, Michaela was adopted and brought to the United States by a couple from New Jersey. She shocked her new mom when she pulled out her picture of the ballerina and said that was what she wanted to be. Her adoptive mom soon enrolled her into ballet school, and by age 20 Michaela had graduated from the American Ballet Theatre's school, danced with the Dance Theatre of Harlem, and appeared on the popular television show, *Dancing with the Stars*. Currently, she is the only dancer of African origin with the Dutch National Ballet. Amazingly, her career is just beginning.

Although Michaela had an adoptive family that loved her unconditionally and was able to support her physical and emotional needs, along the way to manifesting her dream, Michaela met with racial discrimination and discouragement. At age 8, after rigorous practice for the lead role in a juvenile production of *The Nutcracker Suite Ballet*, she was told by a dance instructor right before the show, "People aren't ready for a Black ballerina in the lead role." Then she was told that she didn't have the right body to become a professional dancer. This is a common bias and lie used to discourage Black children from pursuing classical ballet.

Despite these challenges, in April of 2013, Michaela was included in *Newsweek* magazine's international list of the *125 Women of Impact*. Along with the support of a loving family, Michaela has achieved her dream through her courage and willingness to believe in her dream, her faith in her desire for fulfillment in life, and her patient endurance to go through the process. Despite the horrifically tragic deaths of her birth parents, they did not die in vain. Michaela is their happy ending.

# Fairytales Don't Lie

Have you ever stopped to think why fairytales and fantasy stories that use a similar format are so popular in modern culture today? There is no shortage of fairytales, from television series like *Once Upon A Time*, to live action films about Cinderella and Sleeping Beauty, to computer-generated animation films about the Snow Queen, which the high-grossing Disney film *Frozen*, with the Academy Award-winning song, "Let It Go," is a retelling. Of course, I must also include the globally acclaimed *Lord of the Rings* trilogy, and the cinematically unprecedented *Harry Potter* films. So, what's going on? My theory is that with so much chaos, complexity, and technology in our daily lives, not to mention the relentless broadcasts of violent bad news, people are hungry for uplifting reminders about universal truths. Fairytales provide that. Every one of them includes some or all of the following cosmic messages:

- as a human, you are here on Earth to evolve
- trouble and challenges are required for growth and evolution
- help will always come when you call for it and believe you deserve it
- good always triumphs over evil
- there are unhappy consequences for making wrong decisions
- your dreams can come true.

This is why bedtime stories are so important for children. Classic tales like *Hansel and Gretel*, *The Ugly Duckling*, or *The Lion, the Witch, and the Wardrobe*, all seed the developing brain of a child with how the Universe really works. Classic stories connect us to our souls. Every time a child hears about a happy ending, they become more able to believe in that for themselves.

There was a time in the 1970s when fairytales were considered harmful to children. This was during the time of political correctness, where society was waking up to the psychological impact of bias and oppression. In addition to the argument that fairytales were setting children up for great disappointment in life by promoting the notion of living happily ever after, there was also talk of them being too violent, too sexist, and too unrealistic. Thank goodness for the child psychologists who argued back that storytelling is presenting universal symbols and archetypes that are essential for helping children to mentally navigate through life.

Fairytales help children understand the difference between good and evil, while consistently demonstrating that problems can be solved, and that joy and happiness can always be reclaimed. I really think it was that annual television broadcast of the 1939 movie of *The Wizard of Oz*, usually a family event, which so reminded us "Baby Boomers" of the healing power of a great universal story, a story that transcends race, gender, religion and culture, to help us connect with our souls. In this way, we easily can remember the essential cosmic truth —that happy endings are our destiny.

Oh, if you are feeling or being discouraged right now in the pursuit of your heartfelt wishes, authentic dreams, or sacred callings, I highly recommend watching Jiminy Crickett, in the Disney film *Pinocchio*, sing "When You Wish Upon A Star." There's a real good reason why it won the 1940 Academy Award for Best Song. Even now I tear up when I hear it. Cosmic truth and things that connect me to my soul always do that to me.

*When a star is born*
*They possess a gift or two*
*One of them is this*
*They have the power to make a wish come true*

*When you wish upon a star*
*Makes no difference who you are*
*Anything your heart desires will come to you*

(*When You Wish Upon a Star,* music and lyrics by: Ned
Washington and Leigh Harline)

# It's Never Too Late for a Happy Ending: My Happy Ending Story

I am a classical pianist. It's only recently that I have been willing to say that out loud, and to share it with people who thought they knew me. You see, there was a time when my dream of being that was in danger of never coming true. From my story, you'll see that our dreams can be altered so that fulfillment comes to us in the most unexpected and miraculous ways.

I started learning to play piano when I was in the second grade, and from that time on until I graduated from college, I practiced and played religiously for hours every day. Music was in my family. My maternal great-grandfather played the piano and seven other instruments. My grandmother played piano, and so did my mom. To keep up the tradition, my mom bought a Wurlitzer spinet from Gimbels department store. That piano saved my life through adolescence. I wasn't ugly when I was playing the piano. In fact, I was as beautiful as the music I made. It connected me to my soul. It was my Friday night date, my very best friend, and the true love of my life.

Naturally, I wanted to become a concert pianist. But, the music teachers my mother could afford never taught me how to properly use my fingers. With my academic record in high school, I was able to get an audition at Boston University's School of Music, which was my dream school. You can't imagine how embarrassed I was sitting at a Steinway Grand piano, never having played on one before, and struggling to push the keys down.

Of course, I didn't get accepted, and went into a very deep depression. I felt my life had ended. If it wasn't for a caring high school teacher, I wouldn't have gone to any college. Despite this huge let down, my relationship with the piano was so solid, that I continued to take lessons. After working for a short period with two teachers, I was finally led to the woman who finally taught me how to use my fingers, Mrs. Ada Korf.

Mrs. Korf was an amazing human being. Her father was a concert pianist in Poland, who immigrated to the United States to escape the Nazi invasion. He had trained his daughter to become a concert pianist as well. At the age of 15, Mrs. Korf could play of all Beethoven's piano concertos by heart. Her father would also wake her up in the middle of the night, and have her sit and play piano, telling her that she had to be able to perform under any circumstance. When she turned 18, she was one of only two piano students selected for entry into the famous Julliard School of Music in Manhattan. By the time I met her she had already had a very successful career as a concert pianist, touring around the world, and was now settled into teaching at the Manhattan School of Music, and caring for her family.

The first time I met Mrs. Korf I was 19 years old and had never experienced a wealthy home on Manhattan's upper Eastside, which is where she lived. (For those of you who know Manhattan, it was an old money apartment building near the corner of 3rd Avenue and 79th Street.) So, entering the building and being greeted by a doorman was intimidating enough to a middle class, ugly duckling Black girl from Staten Island. Stepping out of the elevator into a foyer with only two doors, knocking on one, and having a maid welcome me into one of the most stately and beautiful rooms I'd ever seen in my life, was downright terrifying!

The living room was wide and decorated in the Georgian style of the 1700's, with Chippendale furniture. It dropped down a step, and there in front of magnificent bay windows were not one, but two grand pianos. (For those of you who know pianos, one was vintage Steinway and the other vintage Mason & Hamlin!) In my mind, my pain body was saying, "Who do you think you are that this woman would take you on as a student? Are you crazy?"

Thank God Mrs. Korf was the kind of person she was. I had been referred to her by a professional jazz pianist who took lessons from her to improve his technique, and he had told her of my love for classical music. She greeted me very warmly and asked me to play something for her on one of those intimidating, top-of-the line pianos. I struggled through *Liebestraum* by Franz List, knowing that she was going to tell me to just give up thinking I could play the piano well enough to call myself a pianist. It took everything to fight back the tears.

When I played the final note, and looked up from the keyboard, she told me to come and sit by her. She looked at me sweetly and told me that I had great musicality, that I truly could feel and understand the language of music. Then she calmly asked me, "Did anyone ever teach you how to use your fingers?" The tears of embarrassment and shame caught in my throat, and all I could do was put my head down and shake it into a "no." Her reply changed my life forever. She said, "Well, I'm going to teach you!"

For the next three and a half years, weekly, I was given not only instruction on the proper use of fingers, wrists, shoulders and arms, but I was given much needed validation and inspiration. Mrs. Korf taught me to let go of needing to be a concert pianist in the traditional way. She taught me to be a concert pianist for myself. She also prophesized that I would use my love and understanding of music to help people. Most importantly, Mrs. Korf was patient, kind and loving to me at a time when I needed it most. She was my first real mentor, and I will treasure her piano lessons and life lessons always.

After graduating from college, I got a job immediately, and for the first time I got a social life. I quietly discontinued taking piano lessons and put all of my attention on being a career woman out to save the planet. At one point in my early career, I bought a beautiful Baldwin concert vertical piano, but ended up donating it to a music teacher in Toledo, Ohio, when my fortunes changed, and I moved on to my next work adventure.

That was back in 1992. Fast forward to 22 years later, when I am visiting at the home of my friends in Wausau, Denise and John Sullivan, who own a beautiful antique upright piano. I began to play again and realized how much I missed this form of expressing myself. Although I would always play any piano in the home of people I knew or was visiting, I still wasn't believing that a piano could come into my life again. I'd spent so much time and energy on helping other people "put on their oxygen masks", that I had neglected remembering to put on mine first!

So finally, I sent out an intention to the Universe that I was ready for piano to come back into my life, by any means necessary. I began to learn the song, "Dawn" from the soundtrack of the Keira Knightly film version of *Pride & Prejudice,* after Denise shared the film, the CD, and the sheet music with me. That lovely piece of music enchanted me, and it called forth my musicality and artistry in a most profound and beautiful way.

What happens next is the icing on the cake. A month later, I'm in Cincinnati visiting with a dear friend and colleague, Quanita Roberson, and we go out to Half Price Books store and I noticed that right next door is a music store. You have to understand, that nowadays it is a rare occasion to find any music store still in operation. So, I knew right away that this was a blessing.

When I entered the store, I was in Heaven! Not only was there lots of sheet music, and classical music books, but not one, but two rows of the most fabulous and beautiful Steinway and Boston Baby Grand pianos! I bought the "Pride and Prejudice" sheet music immediately, then asked the owner if he rented out practice rooms, and how much he would charge. He responded that he had no problem with me coming in the morning to play in one of the rooms. There would be no charge. Fabulous!

So, the next morning I go to practice and play "Dawn." The second day I'm in the practice room for only 15 minutes when the owner knocks on the door. He tells me that I can go play on the grand pianos in the concert room in the back of the store. Well, my heart skipped a beat, and before I knew it I was in the inner sanctum of the Holiest of Holy Realms, playing "Dawn" on a STEINWAY GRAND PIANO!! As fate would have it, Steinway headquarters in New York City was touring three of their treasures around the country. They had all been used by famous pianist like Lang Lang, Diana Krall, McCoy Tyner, and Billy Joel.

As a result of this experience, when I decided to try living in the sun of Phoenix, Arizona, one of the first things I did was to locate a Steinway piano store. I called and spoke with the store manager, Mr. Larry Bateman, asking if there were any practice rooms. He hesitated and then for no reason asked if I was from out of town. After I replied "yes", he told me I could come in and play in his recital hall for one day after 11am. I went the very next day and got to play a Steinway concert grand piano, Model D! After three hours of submerging myself in practicing scales and arpeggios, then playing the pieces I'm working to perfect, I came out of the recital hall and was greeted by Larry. His face was beaming with a smile as he said, "You just bought yourself a ticket to come back and play anytime the room is available."

My dream of being a concert pianist may have been altered, but thanks to Mrs. Korf, the Willis Music Company, my new best friend, Larry Bateman, and my never letting go of my musicality and love of the piano, I have experienced a huge happy ending. Now my new dream is to own a Steinway or Mason & Hamlin Grand piano and return to practicing and playing on a daily basis — until the day I die. I may even enroll in a local music school and take more lessons. In any event, I know that happy endings and fulfillment in life are my destiny — by any means necessary.

# Chapter 4

# Self-Mastery Will Set You Free

## Knowing Your True Self

When you don't know that your true destination in life is to experience your happy endings, then you don't know your true self. To not believe you are worthy of joy, peace and happiness means that your true self is being overshadowed by your pain body – the embedded emotional pain of the past. The great news is that you are not your pain, and your true self never dies. So I thought it would be important to begin this chapter by first sharing my beliefs about the true Self. If we're going to learn to be a master at being the true Self, we need to have a clear understanding of what that is.

In 7th grade, I had a "hippie" English teacher named Mr. Glassman. He was so cool and wore jeans, and all my classmates liked him. Now, Mr. Glassman sincerely wanted to expand the developing minds of preadolescents in deep ways. He was the first adult who ever asked me, "Do you know who you are?" At the time his question confused and frightened me. It felt like he was giving me and my classmates a quiz we hadn't practiced for and were doomed to fail. That wasn't fair.

I don't remember what I said in response to his question -- not that he expected one, but I'm sure it was quite superficial. At age 12, I was still dependent upon the temporal, ever-changing things outside of myself in order to know myself. With that question, Mr. Glassman had given me my first opportunity to begin to question what I believed about myself. Unfortunately, my preadolescent mind believed he knew something about me I didn't know, and I felt ashamed. I also interpreted his asking that question as him telling me, indirectly, that there was something wrong with me. There had to be something wrong, because I really didn't know who I was.

Today, I would respond to Mr. Glassman, "*I am remembering the truth of who I really am every day, and I need the help of you and others to reflect back to me what I unconsciously believe about who I am, so if it's not the truth then I can shift it.*"

The answer to who you are can be done at a very superficial level, based on the temporary things in life like your age, your job, your personal relationships, the roles you play in society, or even how much money you do or don't make. For the purpose of self-mastery, you'll need to answer Mr. Glassman's question at a very deep level, as I have done as an adult.

You see, I believe that as humans, we are here on this Earth and in this third dimensional experience in order to evolve. I believe we are supposed to evolve into people who are masters at knowing how to give and receive love. I believe that as humans, we are divine aspects of a Greater Order and Direction, worthy of love, peace, joy, and happy endings. I also believe that the true self can never be destroyed, no matter how much trauma, drama, or negative circumstances come into our lives. It's always waiting for us to evolve our consciousness enough to be able to identify with our divine truth, rather than our earthbound pain.

In the next section I will write about knowing yourself from the inside out. Please understand, that essentially, I'm talking about knowing how one does and does not love oneself. In addition, it's also important to know the blocks unconditional self-love. Self-knowledge and self-love are essential to attracting and forming healthy and loving relationships. When I meet someone for the first time, I don't care about their race, age, gender, sexual orientation, facial features, hair style, bank account, college degrees, or what kind of car they drive. What's most important to me is whether or not we can lovingly support each other in the truth of who we are.

For example, I once had the most amazing experience regarding my belief in the true Self when I was doing some consultant work with a wonderful group of young people who were living in an intentional community outside of San Francisco. I was at a luncheon in the main house on this beautiful wooded property, and in attendance was a man who looked homeless and messy. His clothes were worn and stained, and his faced showed the lines of a pain-filled life. He didn't look like the kind of person with whom you would want to have a conversation.

He came over to me as I was eating and began to talk with me about books written by shamans that contained beautiful poetry and poetic styles of writing. He had a very soft voice and his approach to me was very gentle and respectful. His name was Peter, and he ended up giving me one of the most profound, and loving lectures about shamanism and indigenous wisdom that I've ever experienced. He was a walking encyclopedia of knowledge. I was open and so grateful to receive his teachings, and we remain friends forever. The old adages are so true: "Never judge a book by its cover!", and "The Truth shall set you free!"

## Knowing Yourself from the Inside-Out

You are truly a slave to painful people, situations, places, thoughts, and ideas, when your pain body is in charge of your life. It will always feel like someone or something is out to get you. You'll believe that no matter how kind and good you are to others, they're never as kind and as good to you. You will effortlessly attract pain into your life and teach yourself to identify with it. Even if you know on an intellectual level that happy endings are your destiny, your pain body will take you to spaces and places to prove you wrong. Of course, all of this is going on at a very deep and unconscious place inside of you. I call this place your 'inner landscape' or 'innerscape.'

As I said previously, your inner landscape is similar to an external landscape, in a symbolic way. Your inner world has mountains and valleys, forests and open fields, rivers, seas, and oceans, as well as lush green playgrounds, and desolate, fallow deserts. These symbolic features of your innerscape will be determined by your inherited ancestral belief systems, the culture of your family of origin, and your early childhood experiences --including your core wound. People who experience much trauma as children may have very challenging innerscapes, with hard to climb mountains, or dark and scary forests through which it is difficult to journey. But, despite however uninviting your inner landscape may be, unlike an external landscape, you have the power to remodel, redesign, reshape and reinvent your landscape. Even better is that you can do all that without having to use a backhoe or power drill.

This essentially is what a healing process does. It brings change to your inner world. All you have to do (*and yeah, I'm kind of being sarcastic here*) is to be willing to journey through your innerscape, confront your pain body, connect with your soul, and transform your emotional pain. This is really hard work, but the rewards are worth it.

In general, when we are children our experience of the world is determined by the people, places, things, and situations around and outside of our innerscape. We are totally dependent upon our external world, and the people in it, for physical and emotional survival. When something goes wrong, like our needs don't get met, or something or someone hurts us, we have no choice but to experience ourselves as victims, and our world as unsafe. As adults, we can learn to respond to our problems, needs, and painful situations from the inside-out.

In adulthood, all of our problems must be resolved internally before the results can manifest externally.

We possess the power to find treasure in our troubles by perceiving them as messages from our innerscape. The message is always about what inside of us is ready to be healed. Changing our perception of trouble, and putting the focus onto ourselves, we free ourselves from victimhood. We can then take on our healing process, which can also be called the redesigning of our inner landscape.

Absent the conscious awareness to know ourselves and experience our world from the inside-out, when negative unexpected things occur in life, we will revert back to our juvenile state, and try to make others totally responsible for our troubles. We will forget that we have an active pain body that is tricking us into believing we are victims. As a result, we will transfer our pain. Knowing yourself from the inside-out will enable you to transform your pain. You will be able to take on full responsibility for your feelings, thoughts, behaviors, and experience of your external world. In a word, you will be doing self-mastery.

## Knowing What Self-Mastery Is and Isn't

Self-mastery is a practice, a discipline, and ultimately a living art form, that enables you to know what it looks like, feels like, tastes like, sounds like, and even smells like when your pain body is attempting to take control of you. Self-mastery is being conscious enough of when you are about to transfer your pain, so you can transform it instead. Self-mastery is the power to control your feelings, thoughts and behaviors when you have been triggered by pain from the past. Here's a short personal example of what I'm talking about.

As I shared in Chapter 2, my core wound is the belief I'm a burden. The pain of this was triggered when I was living as a nomad and visiting with a married couple. They asked me to leave their home earlier than I had originally planned. They told me they needed some time alone, and that was all they told me. My first reaction was shock, and then I fell into my 'poor me' control drama and felt totally victimized. I left early the next day, doing my best to hide my anger, shame and feelings of betrayal, while saying goodbye.

About 50 miles down the road in my car, I decided to stop driving angry, and began to practice self-mastery. As I contemplated what had really occurred, and accepted that my pain body had been triggered, I started to cry. I mean it was a good, deep cry with lots of tears and snot. After my release, I realized that I had unconsciously believed that I was a burden to them for my entire visit.

I was ashamed about not having my own home. My pain body had been telling me that I shouldn't be depending upon the hospitality, generosity and kindness of friends and family. I was telling myself that I should have my own place and that I should be more responsible for my life. I was doing an awful lot of 'should-ing' on myself. The married couple needing time alone had nothing to do with me. By the time I had arrived at my next destination, I was able to call them, and I sincerely thanked them for their hospitality. I was able to appreciate the courage it took for them to be honest with me, and to take care of themselves.

Within six months, I learned that this couple
decided to separate. Self-mastery had freed me
up from taking on their pain.

Self-mastery births your ability to be in control of yourself
and to love yourself unconditionally. You will not be easily
swayed by what other people think, say, or do. You will not
compare yourself to others. You'll know that comparison
doesn't make sense, and that when you do it you will always
come up short, because everyone is unique. You'll spend more
time learning about your uniqueness than trying to figure out
how to be like, or compete with, someone else. You'll no longer
live through your juvenile belief in victimhood. Although you
may have an experience where you react as a victim, you know
you can transcend that belief, and find the true treasure in
your troubles.

Self-mastery is also a very disruptive yet necessary ability
for any human to have. You won't get free of the hold that your
pain body has on you without self-mastery. The paradox is that
being in control of your pain and loving yourself unconditionally
will automatically make you a rebel. Here's why: at this time
on our planet, most people have not mastered themselves.
Most people do not love themselves unconditionally. We live
in a world where going along with the *status quo*, or what is
expected, popular, and easily understood, enables you to be
one of the "in crowd".

Going along with what is expected can also bring social and
financial success. Most people are constantly seeking ways to
fit in, win approval, and be accepted by others. Most people do
not want to deal with their emotional pain, and are constantly,
and unconsciously, transferring their pain to everyone with
whom they come into contact. But if you're reading this book,
you must be willing to learn how to be a self-master. So, below
is a list of examples that will help you understand more clearly
what self-mastery isn't, and what it is.

# What self-mastery is not:

- **Co-dependency:** making someone outside of your Self responsible for whether or not you like or love yourself
- **Control Dramas:** needing to be in some type of control of everybody and everything around you in order to feel safe and secure
- **Victim Consciousness or Taking on Other People's Pain:** being in reaction to the negative things that people say or do; judging and blaming; playing the martyr
- **Manipulation:** any attempt to control anyone but yourself
- **Staying Stuck in the Past:** holding onto people, relationships, situations, and beliefs that can no longer serve you, or support the truth of who you are
- **Taking Revenge:** is what Buddha called picking up a hot coal to throw at someone — you only end up hurting yourself. This is cowardly behavior because it takes courage to turn the other cheek

**Any behavior that is unloving to yourself, or others, is not self-mastery.**

# What self-mastery is:

- **Interdependency:** the ability to support others in the truth of who they are, and expecting them to do the same for you; being fully responsible for whether or not you love yourself
- **Trust and Faith:** trusting yourself and the Universe to keep you safe; knowing that the only person you can control is yourself
- **Victor Consciousness or Taking on Your Own Pain:** the ability to respond to negativity from others with

introspection, acceptance of your pain body, and compassion for yourself and others

- **Being Present:** letting go of whatever is blocking you from being in gratitude, and holding the belief that everything is happening in the right way, and in the right time; knowing you are enough, and worthy of your happy endings in life

- **Practicing Forgiveness:** letting go of wishing for a different past and releasing yourself from carrying someone else's pain; letting yourself off the hook for identifying with your pain, or the pain of others

**Any behavior that is loving to yourself, and others, is self-mastery.**

## Personal Sovereignty: The Fruit of Self-Mastery

Personal sovereignty is *our supreme and independent power over, and responsibility for, our beliefs, thoughts, choices, and their consequences.* Personal sovereignty is the courage to know that the external world is a great mirror of our vast and mysterious inner world. As adults, all that can show up in our life is what we believe about ourselves. What I mean by this is, that the way in which we experience our life will depend upon what is going on in our unconscious innerscape.

As I've mentioned previously, your core wound and the resulting pain body, can have you believing all kinds of lies about yourself and others. When we shift our beliefs and perceptions, our judgements and fears, our experience of people and situations will shift as well. Personal sovereignty is the ability to make that shift from a negative to a positive.

The practice of self-mastery naturally results in our ability to exercise our personal sovereignty. Since the beginning of human time, humans have believed in, and practiced ways, to oppress the human rights of others. The belief that individuals have the ability and birthright, to live freely and cooperatively, is relatively new. Still, as humans, there is something ancient and inherent that we understand about the desire and ability to govern our inner landscape, and not leave that for someone else to do. In general, children at the age of two or three begin to express their desire for personal sovereignty. It's not unusual to hear them say, "I want to do it myself." Even at such an early age, there is the desire to take on responsibility for oneself.

When you can be conscious of your pain body, your victim consciousness, and your control dramas, you will be freed up from giving your personal power over to others in order to survive, and feel safe, liked, and loved. You won't allow yourself to go into or stay in reaction to other peoples' pain. You'll be able to hold your center in the face of life's storms and chaos, as well. It's important to remember, that you cannot be personally free by trying to control, manipulate, or oppress anyone else. You'll experience a 'civil war' within your inner landscape, because your soul knows that personal freedom is not achieved through fear, but only through love.

# Chapter 5

## Healing is a Choice

### Healing Doesn't Feel Good: My Recall Story

*J* first became aware of the fact that I was living with post-traumatic stress symptoms after I had recall of sexual abuse. My recall, or sudden awareness of lost memories, was the experience of lightning out of a clear blue sky. I was totally transformed in an instant. My ego was destroyed. Everything I knew about myself was not to be trusted. I felt bad. Really bad!

My recall was a life-changing event that happened on day two of a three-day personal leadership development workshop called *Transformational Leadership Quest*. I had turned 40 that year and was living alone and quite comfortably in Milwaukee, Wisconsin. I was working as an organizational development consultant and making more money than ever. The workshop that helped to evolve my life was facilitated by my friend, Queen Noor Jawad. I had helped her out with logistics and promotional details, and she extended an invitation for me to experience her work. I accepted her invitation thinking I'd be a conscious observer who could give her quality assurance feedback. But, God had other plans.

The very first day, I was totally disrupted by a woman who had been sexually abused by her grandfather and a man who shared his trauma of sexual abuse by priests when he was at a Catholic boarding school. The tears I cried as this woman and man exposed their core wounds were not just about compassion. The tears were something else, because I couldn't make them stop. The tears were taking over, and I knew that something wasn't right for me.

When I woke up the next morning, I felt anxious and afraid, and I didn't know why. I clearly remember saying this prayer as I stood in front of the mirror in my bathroom, having just put on my lipstick, *"Lord, enable me to receive your blessings, regardless of what form they take!"*

After the completion of the second day, Queen Noor and I met up with our "Waiting to Exhale" sister-girlfriends at one of their homes. We called ourselves that because the film had recently come out and we were six gorgeous, single, and powerful Black women in leadership positions in Milwaukee. All of us were committed to excellence and change. We'd meet every Friday to go out for drinks and dinner and share our work battles of the week. Our meet up was truly about loving and supporting each other. The sight of us together often turned heads, as we represented in real-life the spirit of that groundbreaking film.

In the gathering after the session that day, I remember being seated on the living room floor, recounting what I had experienced during the workshop. As I shared about the two people who had been sexually abused, something came true for me, and I stopped in mid-sentence and said, *"I'm one of them!"* The reaction from my friends was not a reaction at all, but a calm acceptance of *"of course you are!"* Clearly, my woundedness had been much more evident to others than to myself, which is always the case. **Bam!** I now got it intellectually that I was a sexual abuse survivor.

That night was one of the worst nights of my entire life. During that night is when I got it emotionally and physically. My post-traumatic stress symptoms were like thieves that came in the night and stole two of my most valuable belongings — my ability to feel safe, and my self-compassion. For the first time, I realized that my episodic dreams, that I had since childhood, of being chased by monsters into space were rooted in my trauma. I woke up with heart palpitations, cold sweat, and the most horrid feelings of terror imaginable.

Although I got a flash of the face of the person who transferred their pain onto me in my innocence, I did not have memories of what actually occurred. I was too young at the time to have any language for what was happening to me, but that night I experienced phantom pains that were so very real. There was no way I could deny my truth. Through this emotional and physical awareness, so many dysfunctional, out-of-balance, and irrational things in my life began to make perfect sense.

The next morning was a great turning point for me. I knew I could just stay at home and suffer silently, pretending that it would all go away eventually, like a bad dream. I almost did stay home. But something else was at work on my behalf, and a candle I had lit caught fire on the rug in my bedroom. As I scrambled to put it out, and not have the entire rug damaged, the thought flashed in my head, *"You know you're trying to kill yourself!"* It was then that I realized I was not in control of myself, and that I needed help.

I returned to the last day of the workshop, which turned out to be a very positive and empowering experience. We focused on where we wanted to be in 5 years. I wanted to be free of my waking nightmare. Within in two days, I was in therapy, and on serotonin, a mild anti-depression pill. I stayed on serotonin for 1 year and in psychotherapy for two. My life has never been the same. That entire episode brought me to a deep understanding of my true purpose in life: *to heal myself and share my wisdom with others.*

My recall experience was a healing crisis. It didn't feel good, but the results have been miraculous. Usually, when we think of healing, we automatically think of the results. We think of getting back into balance, finding or reclaiming our inner peace, and being relieved from emotional and/or physical pain. The reality is that the only way we get to, "I am healed," is by going through a process. This process is one that doesn't feel good. It's very painful, and I know of at least one major reason why the healing of emotional pain is so painful. Pain from the past, embedded pain, has to be consciously felt and experienced in order to be released. If you can't feel it, have an awareness of it, you can't release it.

Our brains are designed to protect us from fully experiencing pain at the time when it happens. We can shut ourselves down and go numb to it to survive. When the time is right, and you are truly ready, only by sitting in it, and being present to it, can you choose to eliminate embedded pain from your life.

It is hard to have patience for the healing process, but pain that has been repressed for many years will not get released over night. My recall experience was a cracking open to my healing/release process. I prayed for it to be as gentle as possible, and the serotonin helped. There were times when I just wanted it done and over with. I hated having to feel all that yucky stuff. Often, I thought, "This is what it must feel like having to go through a swamp with alligators all around!" Looking back on the life-changing episode now, I'm so grateful that my release process happened over a period of years and in small stages.

I was very fortunate to work with psychotherapists who knew how to hold space for me to do my work, and the right ways to encourage me to keep going forward. After six months of the initial cracking open period, I was able to begin experiencing the initial results of my healing process. I'd get more access to my joy, my confidence, and my clarity about my life. Then, when I was strong enough, the Universe would send me another helping of healing medicine through evolutionary teachers, and situations (also known as "triggers"). So then, I'd sit and release some more. I learned that the pain of the healing process isn't designed to break you. It's designed to break you open so you can break up the pain and have a break through.

I've often said that I wouldn't wish my recall, and painful

aftermath, on the Boogey Man! But, as Maya Angelou wrote, *"wouldn't take nothin' for my journey now,"* because I am freer, emotionally stronger, wiser, more compassionate, and more loving. This is the gift of having sat in my pain and transformed it. So, if you are reading this and going through your own healing crisis, I advise you to throw out the clock! Have patience with yourself and respect the process. Remember, happy endings are your destiny!

## Nobody Can Heal You But You

Most of the time I call myself a healer, but that's not entirely true. I'm more like a facilitator of healing, because I create a safe and loving environment for people to access their own healing power. The power and energy, for healing and transforming pain into joy, resides within every human being. It's part of how we're made. Notice how a healthy body knows how to automatically go to work repairing a cut or bruise. Even when someone has a life-threatening disease, like cancer, their body still goes to work to try and heal them. It's no different with our emotional wounds. More than our psyche and neural networks of our brain are involved. The entire Universe conspires to get us to the right people, places, and situations, at the right time, so that we can make a choice for healing. That is certainly what happened for me. I thought I was moving to Milwaukee for work. I didn't know that the real work was working on my pain.

Over the years I have found that knowing that you have the power and choice to heal yourself is crucial— especially when you are seeking out professional practitioners to help you with your process. When we are at the very beginning of our healing journey, we really need support and guidance. It's a most vulnerable time, and we're stepping into a very mysterious and unknown territory. Rather than making the practitioner responsible for what only you can do, you can be more discerning with whom you work. In other words, you can choose the help you need based upon your specific needs, likes, and dislikes. In this way, you can avoid wasting time working with the wrong persons.

The healing process truly is a life-long journey, and the longer we walk the path to our happy endings, the sweeter and richer it all becomes. Along the way we'll meet people who will dump their pain on us, and also people who know how to lift us up and inspire us. Eventually, we appreciate both the good and the bad, because our souls will expand as a result of both. Eventually, when we get triggered, what used to require days, weeks or even months to get through, will take no more than the time it takes for us to express a sigh. Now that's truly worth all the time and hard work of our healing process.

## *Healing Requires Surrender*

Now that I've talked about healing as a painful process, and a powerful in-born energy, I want to share the most important choice we have to make in order to make it all the way through a healing process. We have to choose to surrender.

Surrender is usually associated with weakness. Not in this case. It takes an awful lot of courage and faith to give yourself over to healing your core wound, and the pain attached to it. I don't know anyone who would choose to dive head first into the depths of emotional pain. I believe the Universe kind of pushes us in, when the time is ripe and right. Still, we live in a free-will Universe, meaning no matter what situation we find ourselves in as adults, we can always choose how we want to react or respond. I've known quite a few people who were pushed into the deep end of their emotional pain pools, but who chose to go into denial, go into judgement and blaming, or to heavily sedate themselves with drugs, alcohol, food, gambling, and shopping, or other addictive behaviors. Until someone is tired enough of their pain, and courageous enough to surrender, the healing process will be put on hold.

I want to write a word or two about how to surrender. I've worked with several people who honestly didn't know how to surrender. Usually these are people who had been conditioned, as children, to believe in a God who was a judge and an executioner. Who'd want to surrender to that? Not me! You see, when I'm talking about surrendering to the healing process, I'm talking about surrendering to a Greater Order and Direction who loves you unconditionally, and who only wants you to have your happy endings come true. So, if you are like these folks and can't surrender to your God because of fear, then surrender to your Soul, your Higher Self. It knows how to be peaceful, joyous, happy and fulfilled, and it wants you to experience that. Saying "YES" to that true part of yourself is surrender. Saying "NO" to your pain body is surrender. Choosing to let go of fear, and to stop running from your pain, is surrender. Getting prostrate on the floor, arms stretched out, hands open and saying aloud, *"I receive, I receive, I receive; thank you, thank you, thank you,"* is surrender.

And once you've surrendered, God—the Universe, all the loving entities of the Cosmos, will take you safely through the healing process. They'll bring you into a wholeness and happiness that you never could have imagined. All you've got to do is choose to let go of what you think you know. Trust your unique healing process. Oh, and there's no monetary charge for theses blessings. It's your birthright.

# Part Two

# Ancient African Wisdom
# for Transforming Pain

# Chapter 6
# The Dagara Medicine Wheel

## The Call of the Ancestors

The Dagara Tribe, of the country known as Burkina Faso (*Land of the Great Ancestors*) in West Africa, has a culture that is many thousands of years old. We call cultures that span the length of known human history "indigenous." Before the wars and civil battles that have resulted from the 400-year period of the Atlantic Slave Trade and European colonialism, the Dagara culture flourished throughout what Europeans called "The Gold Coast" of West Africa. Despite the spread of organized religions like Islam and Catholicism, the Elders of the Dagara communities found ways and means to hold onto their ancient beliefs, practices, and wisdom.

For many centuries, the ancient wisdom of the Dagara provided them with very powerful tools and technology for healing and human evolution. Their wisdom is a technology just like the computer and other essential electronic media is to us. It supported their quality of life. In this twenty-first century, quantum and theoretical physicists are just "discovering" universal truths which the Dagara and other indigenous peoples have known for many lifetimes. For example, within the Dagara creation story, also called a *cosmogony*, you will find elements of the "Big Bang" theory, parallel universes, and the theory of evolution.

I first learned about one of the essential tools in the Dagara cultural medicine bag in the year 2000. That was when I first met Malidoma and Sobonfu Somé. Burkina Faso is the homeland they were called to leave in order to carry their ancient cultural legacy across the Atlantic Ocean to both Europe and the United States. Since the early 1990s, both Sobonfu and Malidoma have done international public speaking, written best-selling books, and recorded audio and video presentations of the ancient wisdom they were called to keep and share. In August of 2000, I met them at separate events, only two weeks apart, and my life has never been the same since. You see, we had never met before, but we recognized each other's soul.

By the year 2008, I was given the opportunity to integrate the technology of the Dagara Medicine Wheel into a human services program for men with embedded childhood trauma. Integrating spirituality into human services had been a dream of mine for 13 years, ever since I fully woke up to walking a spiritual path through life. I didn't know that it would be the Dagara Medicine Wheel, the Alma Center in Milwaukee, or men on probation, who would enable me to live my dream.

## Modernity Is Just Beginning

Before I share just exactly what the Dagara Medicine Wheel is, and how it supports human healing and growth, I must first talk about how this technology came into being. To do that, you need to first know a bit about the indigenous tribal view of the world and the Universe.

The modern conveniences of Western and westernized cultures, that we take for granted, are really not that old. My mother was born in 1933, and she and her siblings grew up in a tin shack out in the country, with no running water and a pot belly stove for heating the three rooms of the shack. They had to manually draw water from a well, used an outhouse for their toilet, and bathed in a metal tub in the kitchen. They grew their own vegetables and killed and ate their chickens. It's only been since the late 19th century that modern times began to exist.

Before the creation of the steam engine and industrialism, humans in the Western world had to deal directly with Nature — and on a daily basis. It is very difficult for those of us enjoying the convenience of supermarkets, microwave ovens, central heating and air, automobiles, Amazon Prime, Smart phones, and Netflix, to imagine how the Dagara Tribe of West Africa was able to survive without any of that.

Like all indigenous or "first people" tribes, the Dagara did not read, write, or do complex mathematics. But they survived for thousands of years, facing all kinds of weather, natural disasters, extreme Earth changes, and even the devastating, unbridled violence and brutality of European imperialism. They survived it all without the support of books, computers or CNN! Once, while visiting with a friend who has teenagers, a summer storm caused a power outage. You should have seen those teens 'climbing the walls' because they couldn't use their electronic media devices. It had only been two hours of no electricity and they were totally in a panic.

## The Indigenous Worldview

So, what is it that has enabled indigenous people like the Dagara to remain alive on this planet without modern conveniences? To put it very simply, it is their belief in, and reverence for, the co-existence of the physical and spiritual worlds. The indigenous worldview, their understanding of the nature of the Earth and the Universe, is rooted in spirituality -- *the awareness of and caring for one's soul.* Today we use the phrase 'finding your spiritual path', but to the Dagara and other indigenous people, *being alive means walking a spiritual path.*

Spirituality for most indigenous people is a cultural expression for living life in a way that brings harmony, peace, and love. Spiritual practices exist to foster and maintain harmonious, peaceful, and loving relationships among humans, and most importantly, between the physical and metaphysical worlds; between that which we can see, hear, touch, taste, and smell, and that which can only be sensed and felt with our heart and soul. Although spiritual practices may be used in fear and anger, in an attempt to control a situation or another person, it was not designed for that. Using spiritual practices out of fear is an aberration, or distortion, of a very sacred technology.

All indigenous spirituality, including African spirituality, is deeply rooted in the belief that the Earth, the oceans, the plants, animals, and all humans, have come from the same Source. There is no separation between humans and the natural world, or the world above our heads. This is in direct conflict with the worldview of modern Western cultural established just in the 17th to 18th centuries during what was called "The Age of Enlightenment." One of the major goals put forth during this time was to conquer Nature. This is the total opposite of what the Dagara and other indigenous people believe. They believe that Nature is to be revered and honored as a divine source from which we can learn how to sustain, heal, and evolve ourselves. This is why the Dagara Medicine Wheel is so important. It is a spiritual tool that enables us to remember and honor our divine connection to the universal elements of fire, water, earth, minerals (stones, bones, and shells), and the evolving entities of nature (plants, animals, and humans).

## The Dagara Creation Story

The origin of the Dagara Medicine Wheel is told through a creation story, also called a *cosmogony*. Most people in Western cultural only know of the story of Adam and Eve, but every indigenous culture has a story of how the Earth, the animals, and humans came into being. The Dagara creation story is an essential part of their oral storytelling tradition. Usually, a drummer would accompany the storyteller to give musical emphasis to the 'call and response' parts of the story. What I'm about to share with you isn't usually written down, but I must share it so that you will have a greater understanding of why and how the medicine wheel provides such powerful healing to those who engage with it. It goes something like this:

Once upon a time; once before time, there was a huge ball of **Divine Fire** flying and traveling through the outer limits of deep space. This divine ball of Fire was traveling tremendously fast -- I mean so fast that no human can ever imagine how fast that ball of fire was going! And, because this Divine Fire was traveling so very, very fast, it actually tore a huge hole into the Other World.

*"The Other World?", you say. "What Other World?"* Well I'm talking about the world that exists right next to ours, but most humans are unable to see it. So, from out of this Other World that the Divine Fire ball ripped opened, poured the most beautiful and precious thing the Divine Fire had ever seen. It was Precious Water, and he fell in love at first sight.

The **Precious Water** fell right into the open arms of Divine Fire, for she had been sleeping for a very long, long time. She woke up with a jerk of her precious head, looked up at Divine Fire and said, "Hey! Who are you?" Divine Fire was so taken over by her loveliness, his heart bursting with passion, that he responded back to his Beloved without blinking an eye, "I've come to marry you, and be with you for eternity!" Precious Water at first was surprised and taken aback, but then she remembered that she had dreamed of him during her long sleep. "Of course," she sighed happily, "let's go fly, sing, dance, and play!"

So Divine Fire and Precious Water began to do their cosmic dance and play all over this Universe. They sang their love songs and rolled all around their eternal space having just a good 'ole time.

(Call) **And you know what happens when Beloveds get to singing and dancing and rolling all around?**

(Response) **Something gets created!**

So, before you know it, Divine Fire and Precious Water gave birth to a new Being. They decided to call their child **Magnificent Earth.**

When the parents of Magnificent Earth first gazed upon their new born, they were overwhelmed with joy, happiness, and gratitude. Divine Fire decided he was going to always watch over and protect Magnificent Earth by placing a part of himself above her and also inside her heart. Precious Water decided she was always going to nurture and caress her child by placing a part of herself over Magnificent Earth like a blanket. Also, because she loved Divine Fire so much, she said that she would visit him above by transforming herself into clouds. She said she would even find pathways into the Earth to support him in her heart.

And so it was that Magnificent Earth was protected and nurtured by Precious Water and Divine Fire. They were truly a happy and loving family, but one day Magnificent Earth grew sad. She was lonely because she didn't have any playmates. When her parents heard her lament, they knew exactly what to do. So, one day they all got together and did a 5-day ritual of singing, dancing and playing.

(Call) **And you know what happens when folks come together to have a good time like that?**

(Response) **Something gets created!**

And so Divine Fire, Precious Water, and Magnificent Earth created **Awesome Minerals,** which took the form of mountains, boulders, caves, rocks, crystals, and sand.

Now Magnificent Earth was so happy and excited to have her first playmates. She was having so much fun all the time now, and she wanted more! So, one day she asked her parents to join her and her Awesome Minerals to create more playmates. Once again, another 5-day long ritual of singing, dancing, and playing was performed.

(Call) **And you know what happens when folks come together to have a good time like that?**

(Response) **Something gets created!**

And so, it was that Divine Fire, Precious Water, Magnificent Earth, and Awesome Minerals created **Bountiful Nature**.

Bountiful Nature took the form of living creatures that could roam and play all over Magnificent Earth. This is why we have the **Healing Plants**, the **Tremendous Trees**, the **Beautiful Flowers**, and the **Amazing Animals**.

With so many playmates and so much fun going on all the time, you can't imagine that Magnificent Earth wouldn't be satisfied. But she wasn't, and she wasn't alone in her feelings. Her mineral and nature playmates also felt that something else was missing. So, once again, a 5-day long ritual was held with such singing, dancing, and playing that no human can ever imagine!

(Call) **And you know what happens when folks come together to have a good time like that?**

(Response) **Something gets created!**

And so, it was at the end of the 5th day of unimaginable joyous ritual that the Divine Fire, the Precious Water, the Magnificent Earth, the Awesome Minerals, and the Bountiful Nature with her Healing Plants, Tremendous Trees, Beautiful Flowers, and Amazing Animals, all created the **Blessed Humans**.

So all of you listening to me right now know this truth of who and what you come from. Remember that you have been loved, sung, danced, and played into existence. Always remember and never forget that you are:

**Divine,**

**Precious,**

**Magnificent,**

**Awesome,**

**Bountiful,**

**Healing,**

**Tremendous,**

**Beautiful,**

**Amazing,**

and,

**Blessed.**

And so it is. Ashé!

# Chapter 7

## The 5 Original People and Their Elemental Portals

### The Sacred Number 5

*I*t is the belief among the Dagara Tribe that every human who is born into this world has their soul infused with one of the five elements of their medicine wheel. In other words, everyone goes through an *elemental portal* on their way to physical and earthly existence. Every child is born imprinted with the essential knowing and genius of their element, which is called *elemental essence*. Each elemental portal holds information on specific gifts and talents, human characteristics, and information for life purpose that no one has to teach you. You are able to know your elemental essence naturally. You are born full.

The number 5 in Dagara culture is very sacred. Unlike the Gregorian and Roman calendars that we use to keep track of days, weeks, months, and years, the Dagara only use the numbers one through five. Our days of the week are named after Greek and Roman gods. For the Dagara, it is the five essential elements for human existence that provide structure and meaning to their experience of daily living.

It's interesting that in the art of numerology (the use of numbers to expand consciousness of life purpose and events) the number 5 denotes "wholeness" and "dynamic force for life". The Dagara belief system teaches that having each of the five elements represented in human form is what creates vitality, diversity, balance, harmony, and peace within the village. It is believed that the five original people of the Earth were born through Fire, Water, Earth, Mineral, and Nature — in that order. Below is information to help you identify your elemental essence, along with descriptions of each elemental portal, and the human characteristics and inherent gifts of each essential element.

## Finding Your Elemental Portal

Below is a chart that provides the numerical system developed by the Elders of the Dagara Tribe to enable those of us living in Western culture to know what elemental portal we were born through. To identify your element, use the last number of your birth year. For example, if you were born in 1957 like me, then you use the number 7, which is the Fire portal. Also, on this chart of elemental wisdom, I've listed the sacred directions and medicine colors associated with each of the elements. I've also referenced the primary purpose and services that each element provides to the community.

| Last number of birth year | 1 or 6 | 2 or 7 | 3 or 8 | 4 or 9 | 5 or 0 |
|---|---|---|---|---|---|
| Element | Water | Fire | Nature | Mineral | Earth |
| Direction | North | South | East | West | Center |
| Medicine Color | Blue/Black | Red | Green | White | Yellow |
| Primary Purpose | Peacemaker | Speaker of Truth (Soothsayer) | Guardian of Cycles of Change | Storyteller & Wisdomkeeper | Guardian of Home, Comfort and Abundance |
| Service to Others | Emotional flow and intelligence | Gatekeeper for the Ancestors | Trickster and Magician | Reminder of & Connector to Purpose | Unconditional love and nurturing |

# The Fire Portal and Fire People

*The first spark of consciousness congealed within the infinite mind of the Divine Creator, and it was Light. Every creation that followed, even the creation of matter, has as its foundation that initial spark of consciousness. The energy of Light is the most powerful force one can call upon when seeking healing or spiritual growth, because it is the foundation of all else in our reality.*
— **Ashian Naisha**, *Crystal Ally Cards - Guidebook*

Fire is the most primal element of the Dagara cosmology. Its power for transformation, which is fast and furious, is the most radical of all the elemental forces. Fire represents the power of the sun and the stars here on Earth. It takes the form of lightning blazing down from the sky, as well as the red hot molten magma of the Earth's subterranean interior. Fire is very impatient and very fast. Whatever comes into contact with Fire will immediately begin to be transformed and transmuted into an unrecognizable shape, texture, and form. It will consume everything in its wake until there is nothing left to consume, or until it is stopped.

In its most loving forms, Fire is the provider of light against darkness, warmth against cold, and a powerful resource for cooking and making metal tools. But, it can become as dangerous and destructive as an out-of-control forest fire, or a raging volcano that spews mega tons of lava and ashes. Although the ferocious nature of fire is to be feared, it is also to be appreciated. Fire's transformational energy eliminates what would block the creation of new growth. Some of the most beautiful places on Earth, places we liken to paradise, like Hawaii, owe their lush green landscapes full of unique and beautiful flowers and fruits, to the eruption of volcanoes.

Fire also symbolizes the doorway between our world and

the Other World where ancestors reside. The Fire Portal is very sacred to the Dagara Tribe because of their belief in ancestors as guides and protectors. The Dagara do not believe in Heaven and Hell like that of the Christian, Islamic, Judaic, or Hindu religions. They believe that when someone dies, their soul must travel back to the *Land of the Ancestors*, which is very much like this world, but without the physical boundaries. In this Land, every soul is returned to its original divine consciousness, and gets to review how much or little of their sacred promises they were able to keep. They are not judged or punished for their behaviors. Whatever happened when one was on Earth is processed, integrated, and used to help those left behind.

## The Essence of Fire People

People born through the Fire Portal are the soothsayers or truth-tellers of the village. Fire people walk a very thin line between this world and the Ancestral realm. As natural keepers of the Fire Portal, they have unfiltered access to what is really going on behind the scenes that others can't or don't want to see. The little child in the fairytale, *The Emperor's New Clothes*, who blurts out the truth that no adult has the courage to say, is definitely a Fire person!

Often, people do not want to see a Fire person coming because of their ability to pull back the curtain or pull off the covers to things and truths that others would rather not have exposed or brought out into the open. It can be very difficult for a Fire person to keep their mouth shut when they know a truth. The African adage of, *"If you're going to speak the truth, be sure to have your horse by the door,"* is very good advice for Fire people. As adults, Fire people must learn to practice being diplomatic and considerate. They must learn patience for the right timing for sharing the truth.

In addition to their soothsaying, Fire people also possess

natural and visionary leadership ability. With their pioneering spirit, they are not afraid to lead the way through unchartered territory, or as we say, "blaze a trail." The primal energy of Fire makes them excellent at getting things started and heated up, and they will keep the momentum going until the process can run on its own. Fire people are highly intuitive, and easily interpret dreams and situations that others find too confusing. Of course, they are also very passionate about all things being truthful, just, and in right order.

## The Water Portal and Water People

> *Water is one of the crucial materials that our bodies need to sustain life. It is "liquid air", the blood of the Earth, and a powerful source of energy for the cleansing of the heart and emotions. Water is yielding and receptive, yet it can wear down mountains if given time. From this element we learn release, constancy, joy, and the way of Water — going with the flow.*
> — **Ashian Naisha**, *Crystal Ally Cards - Guidebook*

Water is the most mysterious and mutable of the elements. Some scientists now theorize that the Earth's water was brought from *another world* by way of asteroids and comets. As humans, we are essentially water beings. At birth, most babies are 99.5% water. As we age, we begin to lose our water, which is why we get wrinkles. Most people over the age of 70 have about 50% water remaining in their skin cells. Water is a great conductor of energy, like electricity, music, and the resonance of love and fear. It is the water and blood in our bodies that contribute to our experience of emotions.

Water possesses the power to easily and effortlessly change its shape and form, without ever being destroyed. It can make space for, and wrap itself around, whatever object or person comes into its midst. It can take on the shape of any container into which it is poured. Water can effortlessly transform itself from a liquid to a solid block of ice, to a gas, a fog, or a cloud, and then back again to running water.

Water is at its best when it is allowed to flow and find its way back to the ocean as a stream, or a river. When water is blocked, it becomes stagnant and eventually poisonous. When water is flowing, it can purify and revive that which was sick and dying. It can soften and revive things and places that have been dehydrated.

Every living thing requires fresh flowing water in order to survive. This is why water has been called, "the elixir of life."

The transformational power of Water can be as gentle and kind as a misty spring rain, or as calming as a babbling brook deep within a thick forest. Yet, the element of Water can bring about change that is as brutal and unforgiving as a flood or a tsunami. Water is one of the first resources that humans turn to for physical, mental, emotional, and spiritual cleansing. Infants are baptized with it, and adults wanting to be 'born again' are ceremoniously immersed in it. Water has the power to calm, soothe and revitalize.

## The Essence of Water People

Water people are the peacemakers of the village. They are very emotionally sensitive, and like Water itself, they are easily able to take on whatever feelings and energies are around them. This means that they can easily take on carrying other people's pain — especially when it is deeply hidden. The natural ability of Water people to have compassion for others is what enables them to take on building bridges when conflicts occur. They have the power to see beyond the turmoil and anger of a situation and will often take on reconciling what others believe is impossible to reconcile.

Water people can naturally cry very easily. In our culture, we are conditioned to believe that tears are a sign of weakness. But the true gift of tears is that they bring emotional intelligence to situations and people when emotional release and purification is needed. The Dagara elders consider modern Western culture a *"fire culture"*, due to our over consumption of food, water, products, and natural resources. They believe, and I wholeheartedly agree with them, that we are avoiding having to feel our stuck emotional pain, because we've lost the ability to fully grieve. So, Water people are very much needed in our culture. They provide a critical balance to our over-the-top hunger for faster cars, bigger houses, and all the food we can eat!

Through their inherent ability to think first from their heart before their head, Water people are able to demonstrate the importance of choosing Love over Fear. Water people understand love as something that everyone is capable of, and they enjoy connecting people to their hearts, and to the universal power of love. Water people can be depended upon to include love, and the emotions of the heart and soul, in important decision-making and daily living.

## The Earth Portal and Earth People

> The elemental force of Earth is the manifestation of the energy of life. The Earth represents the bones of the Great Mother, upon which all nature is constructed. . . Earth is the basis upon which all of creation is built. It is through her fertility and bounty that the great web of life is spun. This elemental force is the doorway through which all of our own manifestations are born. It is her frequencies and influence that transform energy into matter and lend form to all ideas and endeavors you choose to focus upon.
>
> — **Ashian Naisha,** *Crystal Ally Cards - Guidebook*

Although there is no hierarchy among the elements (no one element is more important or better than another), Earth for plants, animals, and humans is quite essential. Earth provides the physical foundation for the experience of living. The Earth portal represents the creative, fertile, abundant energy of the Universe. Earth is our eternal home.

The Earth element has the power to transform whatever is buried within it, whether that takes a few months, or a few millenniums. It can also birth things and make them grow. Or, it can decay things and transform them back into the dust out of which they manifested. Like Water, Earth is patient with its transformation process — until it needs to lose its patience. That's when it brings about formidable change through the shifting of its tectonic plates, which we experience as earthquakes.

The Earth portal is the portal of manifestation. The energy of the Earth provides everything that is organic, material, and physical in order for us to survive. The Earth also provides us with a place to set our feet upon, to stand up firmly, and to be able to establish a home. It also provides walk ways, trails, passages, and roads for us to journey upon and expand our experiences of being alive. This nurturing and supportive aspect of the Earth is why it is often referred to as "The Great Mother."

## The Essence of Earth People

Earth people are the nurturers and land stewards of the village. They are born with a superhuman understanding of the importance of home, stability, and consistency, in order for humans to grow, develop, and achieve identity in a healthy and loving manner. The primary concern of Earth people is that everyone around them is in physical comfort, well-fed, and grounded. Their heightened physical sensibility enables them to easily feel when someone is in need of nurturing and care.

Earth people will literally give you the shirt off their backs, and they are happiest and at their best when they have pots cooking on the stove, and family and friends around their dining table. Earth people delight in reminding others that there is always enough. They believe beyond a question or a doubt that basic needs are supposed to be met. It hurts them to their core that people experience hunger and homelessness.

The selfless, considerate, and compassionate nature of Earth people makes them very sought out and depended upon. Everyone loves to be welcomed, safe, and nurtured. Earth people know how to create loving family environments and relationships. The father in the parable of *The Prodigal Son* must have been an Earth person, because of his ability to "keep the light on" for his wayward son. This is what Earth people do so well. They empower and validate others with their natural ability for unconditional love.

## The Mineral Portal and Mineral People

*It is the mineral kingdom which makes up the soil of the planet and fills the waters with rich nutrients. It is the mineral kingdom that gives sustenance to the plant kingdom, which in turn sustains the animal and human kingdoms. But the mineral kingdom does much more than simply feed the plants that we eat. Minerals also carry the most important ingredient for life on the planet – energy.*
— **Ashian Naisha,** *Crystal Ally Cards - Guidebook*

Minerals are the first-born children of the Earth. They are natural record- keepers who hold the story of the beginning of the Earth, and all of what the Earth has experienced over millions and millions of years. Minerals can take the form of grains of sands, pebbles and stones, precious gemstones, or gigantic

71

boulders, rolling hills or the majestic Himalayan Mountains, and even the Grand Canyon. The bones of humans and animals are also part of the Mineral kingdom. Just like the stones of the Earth, our skeletal system is encoded with our ancestral history. Past life remembrances are rooted in our bones, passed down from previous generations through the DNA.

The transformational power of Minerals resides in their ability to receive vital and creative vibrations from the Source of universal energies, and to transmit or broadcast that high frequency energy out to every living thing. This is why since ancient times humans have used stones, crystals, and precious gems and metals in spiritual and religious structures and healing practices. Minerals reign supreme in the modern world as well. It is tiny chips of quartz crystal that enable the communication magic of computers, cell phones, and other digital technology.

For most humans, the transformational energy of Minerals is invisible, but all humans have the ability to sense and feel these healing energies through the heart and soul. Because of their high frequency transmissions, Minerals can powerfully awaken and evolve human consciousness. They are very important allies for creating change an invoking transformation from the inside-out.

## The Essence of Mineral People

Mineral people are the wisdom keepers and storytellers for the village. Their natural ability for remembering details, often photographically, enables them to be very talkative. The have the capability to become great communicators, lecturers, and teachers. Mineral people know how to easily make and maintain social connections. This insures that they have a good audience for all of the information and knowledge they have to share. Mineral people love history, and they love to tell stories about history as if they were actually there. Another very important thing that Mineral people find easy to do is help to set ethical and meaningful boundaries and structure to their families, and communities.

Probably the most powerful gift of the Mineral people is their ability to help others remember their purpose for being alive. In the Dagara culture, there is the belief that the most dangerous person in the village is the person who doesn't know, or has forgotten, their purpose. Knowing and living on purpose is understood to be the key to achieving fulfillment in life. Through their keeping of family history, cultural practices and teachings, as well as ancient wisdom stories, Mineral people can always be called upon to help others remember that no human is supposed to be disposable — we are all Divine.

# The Nature Portal and Nature People

*We have all chosen to incarnate on Earth at this time of change in order to bring a remembrance of harmony to humanity. The cancer that humanity's mayhem has created on the planet can only be healed by teaching those who are out of tune with the great song of life to once again move into measure with the natural song of creation. We have come to heal our own discord; and in doing, heal the total being of the Great Earth Mother — planet, plant, animal, human, and spirit.*
**— Ashian Naisha,** *Crystal Ally Cards - Guidebook*

Last but not least, the Nature portal represents the sum total of the other four elemental forces. According to the Dagara cosmology, it's the combination of Fire, Water, Earth, and Minerals that produces, as well as sustains, the plants, the animals, and the humans. The Nature element is all about the evolutionary impulse of the Universe. Through Nature's energy we learn that all plants, animals, and humans are on this Earth to be born, to grow, to mature, to heal, to age, to die, and to evolve. This is what we call 'being alive.' Change is a very natural and necessary part of our experience of living. It is the only constant state of our existence. The reality of change, of life, of death, and rebirth, of beginnings, and of endings, is the powerful transformational energy of the Nature portal.

## The Essence of Nature People

Nature people are the guardians of life and death for the village. They have a natural reverence for change. Nature people inherently understand the need for acknowledging the ending of things with grief, and the need for praising that which is just beginning. They can believe that rain will return after a long drought, when others are hopeless and in despair. It is because of this powerful ability to blindly trust in the reality of change that Nature people are called "tricksters." They are able to sing, dance, and play during tough times, when others think everyone should be fearful and quiet.

Another important gift that Nature people possess is their ability to easily and effortlessly manifest something out of nothing using their deep understanding of change and transformation. They are likened to the alchemists who worked to turn lead into gold. Their inherent manifestation abilities have them known as the witches and wizards of the village. Their love of the natural world, and ability to hear, understand, and speak the language of plants, trees, and animals, also greatly contributes to their mystical and magical reputations.

Nature people are deeply connected to the natural landscape and all its inhabitants. They love and revere the change of seasons, sunrises and sunsets, and change in the weather. Lightning and thunderstorms make them feel alive because it speaks so deeply to their understanding of destruction and creation as two sides of the same coin. Authenticity characterizes Nature people because their connection to the raw, unfettered majesty of Nature makes it difficult for them to be anything else. They know how to promote the importance of authenticity for creating and living in harmony, peace, joy, and fulfillment.

## My Elemental Essence Story

When I first learned that I was a Fire person, I felt a huge relief. I was in my 40s, and it was the first time in my life that I could make peace with myself for being able to see the truth about people and situations, and to speak it aloud. An important aspect of the elemental essence of Fire people is that they are naturally compelled to see and hear the truth, and to share it with everyone around them. During childhood, I was that little child in the fairytale, *The Emperor's New Clothes*. I was always telling on my brother and sister or commenting on things that were better left unsaid. My mother would say that I "talked fresh" or that I had a "fresh mouth." She warned me that my mouth would always get me in trouble.

As I grew up, I did learn that it wasn't polite to say things out loud just because I could. In adolescence, not wanting to be disliked by anyone, I made sure to keep my mouth shut so I wouldn't hurt other people's feelings. I chose diplomacy, but also chose to believe that there was something wrong about my ability to see through the facades of people and situations. Telling and speaking the truth kept me much more isolated than I would have liked. So, I chose to go into denial by telling myself I was making stuff up. Rather than accepting the truth of who or what a person or situation was, I would put myself into a position of expecting the person or situation to be able to do or be for me usually what they could not. I often felt disappointed, betrayed, and victimized.

After learning about my elemental essence, I began to claim my truth-seeing and truth-speaking as a gift. I realized that no one had taught me how to see truth. It was natural for me. This realization helped me stop comparing myself to others, and to believe that I was unique and enough. The trouble my mother was warning me about was really about living my purpose. I decided that I would use my truth-telling to break free from co-dependent relationships. Then I decided to help others who were ready and willing to face their hidden truth, in order to free themselves from painful emotions, relationships, and situations. Today, I am no longer a victim to what is my natural ability. Truth-telling, also called *soothsaying*, is an essential part of my work as a diviner, wisdom consultant, and shamanic healer.

To sum it all up, your elemental essence is the divine gifts, talents, and genius that you received when you emerged into this world through an elemental portal. When you claim your elemental essence as your truth, as your natural self, then you get access to the powerful eternal truths. This divine treasure may not show up in conscious thought or words at first, but your willingness to embrace your elemental essence initiates a vibrational signal to your psyche, and everyone around you. This vibrational signal is invisible and silent, but more powerful than your intellect or any negative beliefs about your Self.

# Chapter 8

## The Five Elemental Forces

$\mathcal{N}$ ow that I've introduced you to the Dagara Medicine Wheel and it's five primal elements, as well as the elemental portals that every human is born through, you're probably wondering how healing comes out of all this. Well, the answer to that requires three more important pieces of Dagara wisdom. The first piece is the belief among the Dagara people that humans are essentially the evolved and evolving expression of the energies and forces associated with each element. The second piece of wisdom is how the 5 elements co-exist in and around your physical body. The third piece is a look at your elemental energies when they are healthy, and when they are unhealthy.

## The Dawn of Life

One of my favorite cable television shows is a documentary series called, *How The Universe Works*. Each episode is filled with lots of mind-blowing information about the formation of stars, planets, galaxies, and life on planet Earth. I love the awesome computer graphics used to illustrate what a very diverse group of scientists teach about on the show. There's one episode that really clicked with me, in relation to the Dagara creation story. It's called, *The Dawn of Life*.

In this episode, the astronomers, astrophysicists, planetary scientists, and theoretical physicists all agree that everything that exists is made up from just a handful of primal ingredients. These original chemicals, like hydrogen, lithium, and helium, are found in plants, animals, dirt and rocks, rivers and oceans, as well as humans. This means that humans are organically and chemically connected to the Universe and everything in it. We all come from the same stuff!

Thousands of years before the modern science theories and discoveries showcased in *How the Universe Works*, the Dagara people were using their medicine wheel to acknowledge, honor, and appreciate the fact that humans are not separate, but are deeply and eternally connected to everything around them. From this perspective, the five elements of fire, water, earth, mineral, and nature are powerful allies for health and wellness. The five elements are our "parental guides' because we are born out of their existence. They are our original Elders, and we can rely upon them to replenish our energy and remind us of the deep truth of who we are —divine beings who belong to a vast and mysterious Universe.

By engaging with the five elements as intelligent and loving Beings who have the energy and ability to be medicine to humanity, the Dagara people were able to develop a technology for healing. This technology involves an understanding of how each of the five elements contributes to our physical body, our emotions, and our spiritual awareness. This ancient information fosters the belief that we are a vital member of the Universe, and the world all around us.

## We Are the Five Elements!

Each of the five elements exists in a physical form, but like all physical things in our Universe, there are also other forms that they can take. Below is a guide to how the elements show up as forces within in and around our human body, and the colors associated with those forces.

**FIRE**: This red elemental force is our spark of life. It is the explosive, electrical energy that runs through every cell, every nerve, every bit of our physical self. Our Fire animates us and gets everything moving. It is the force that beats our hearts, that breathes us, that enables us to think, speak, sing, walk, run, hip hop, and reproduce. The Chinese call this elemental force "Qi" (sounds like *chee*), and they describe it as a flame that sits right behind our belly button. The expression *"fire in the belly"* means having a strong desire or ability to make things happen. That is what the elemental force of Fire does very well.

**WATER**: No living thing can exist without water. Not only do humans develop in their mother's womb in a sack full of water, but at birth, our bodies are made up of about 95% water. We lose water as we age, and that is why our skin will wrinkle.

The blue/black elemental force of water is not just our network of blood vessels and plasma in our cells. It is also the force behind our emotions. This is why crying, or sweating is so important. It is how we know that we have feelings. The elemental force of Water enables us to feel and relate to people, animals, plants, anything we care about. That includes our Self. Without the force of Water, we would not know how to give or receive love.

**EARTH**: The yellow elemental force of Earth takes the form of our skin. This external organ is the protective material that makes it possible for us to experience the three-dimensional reality of our existence. Our skin enables us to touch and be touched. It is our flesh that serves as an essential caretaker of our vital internal organs, like our lungs, kidneys, and heart.

Our skin also provides a home for our soul, or spiritual consciousness. The elemental force of Earth is a protective energy that nourishes and sustains our ability to survive the physical challenges of being alive. In Western culture, a common phrase spoken at burials for someone who has died is, *"ashes to ashes, dust to dust."* This means that our physical body came from the Earth, and to the Earth it will return. Our Earth, in the form of our skin, grounds our soul so we can experience what we came into to this world to do, to have, and to be.

**MINERAL:** The Mineral of our human body is our skeleton. At birth, this system of 270 bones contains the blueprint for our appearance, our brain function, our reproductive ability, and our aging process. Our bones are a library of information and knowledge that is older than the Pyramids, or the ancient library of Alexandria. The white elemental force of mineral enables us to live on purpose. It connects us to the right people, ideas, situations, and environments so we can experience and discover the truth of who we are. The old saying, *"I know it in my bones,"* is a direct acknowledgement of the power of our Mineral.

**NATURE:** Unlike the other four elemental forces, Nature doesn't take on a physical appearance. This green elemental force is the invisible, all-powerful evolutionary impulse of the Universe. Our Nature is the energy that guides our growth and development from birth until death. It is the force that keeps us changing and evolving, whether we like it or not! Nature carries us through the seasons and changing weather of our life. The elemental force of Nature enables us to experience our life as an unfolding, transformational journey. We can never end up the way we began. Our ability to change is involuntary and inevitable. We may resist the process of growing, aging, and dying, but it is quite natural. No human can escape the power of the elemental force of Nature. The question, "what is your true nature," means who are you naturally? Our answer to this will change throughout our lifetime.

# Elemental Forces In and Out of Balance

In addition to the five elemental forces being represented as physical and spiritual aspects of your body, they also serve as metaphysical energy centers. These invisible, yet powerful, energy centers within you can be likened to the power box usually found in the basement or utility room of a home. Inside this box are power switches that control the amount and flow of electricity into the home. When the switches are on, then you get to use your lights, television, and washing machine. If a switch is off, or if it experiences a power surge —too much electricity coming through the lines, then your electrical appliances won't work right, or not at all.

Below is a quick overview of what you can experience when your own elemental forces/energy centers are switched on, meaning that they are in balance and healthy, and what you can potentially experience when they are not.

**Fire Healthy and Balanced:** The best way to describe this is a perfect candle flame, strong, steady, and bright. In this condition you are able to move about easily and effortlessly. You wake up easily in the morning, raring to go and get things going. You also know when things are enough, and you set your limits with all of life's activities, like eating, sleeping, exercising, spending money, socializing, and working. You are able to maintain your energy because you do not over work yourself. You never burn the candle at both ends.

**Your Unhealthy Fire:** When your Fire is too much and out of control, you are like a raging volcano or a forest fire that consumes everything in sight. In this state, you may experience being passively or violently abusive to yourself or others. You may act controlling and intimidating with bursts of anger, rage, hysterical crying, and other forms of dysregulated behaviors. You may experience addictive behaviors with work, food, sex, gambling, shopping, and other ways of not being able to know when enough is enough. You'll be the Energizer Bunny who keeps on going, and going, and going, unable to stop yourself.

When your Fire is too low, like a candle flame that is weak and wavering, you will not have enough energy to move about or do much of anything. In this state, you may experience fatigue, weariness, exhaustion, sleepiness, and depression. Ultimately, through the process of aging, all humans will have their Fire start to go out. Once our Fire is extinguished, we experience death.

**Water Healthy and Balanced:** Water is at its best when it flows gracefully and steadily without being obstructed. A musical mountain stream, an awe-inspiring waterfall, a lazy river, or gentle waves rolling in and out of a shore describe healthy water. In this state, we are emotionally intelligent. We respond with compassion, caring, and tears to things that touch our hearts. We love ourselves unconditionally, and find it easy to be loving, kind, and gentle with other people, animals, plants, and ourselves.

**Your Unhealthy Water:** When your Water is overflowing, behaving like a flood or tsunami, your sad emotions will rule you. You will be raw and like a sponge to the painful feelings of others, as well as your own. In this state, known as "being lost in liquid", you will attempt to sedate the pain with alcohol, pharmaceuticals, injections of heroin or cocaine, or other mind-altering substances. Chronic depression may also give evidence to the overflowing of your Water, and feelings of numbness, apathy, and generally just not caring about yourself, other people, or life itself. Being 'lost in liquid' feels like there's no way out of your misery, so suicide is associated with unhealthy Water.

Water can also not flow at all and become stagnant, like a murky swamp or cesspool. In this state you may experience rigidity in thought and behavior. You may become overly judgmental and critical of yourself and others. Inflexibility and inability to be hopeful or considerate also is evidence of stuck Water. Being unable to feel your emotions of joy and happiness is another sign that your Water is in an unhealthy status.

**Earth Healthy and Balanced:** When you know that you are loved, cared for, appreciated, acknowledged, and as a result you feel happy, satisfied and safe, then your earth elemental force is in balance and healthy. In this state you are able to nurture others, as well as yourself. You have an abundance mentality and live in the flow of reciprocity –letting go and letting come. You trust in the power of God and the Universe to provide for your every need, easily and effortlessly. You are caring, kind, and loving. You are grounded in the belief that you matter, and that you are worthy of your happy endings in life.

**Your Unhealthy Earth:** When your Earth is out of balance it's like a barren desert with nothing living in sight. You do not feel loved, cared for, appreciated, acknowledged, happy, satisfied, or safe. In this state, anxiety and fear rule your world. There is a feeling of "homelessness", of not wanting to be alive. Life is about survival, struggling and suffering. You may be suffering from scarcity mentality, oppressed by growing debt, financially living from hand to mouth, unable to believe that you deserve blessings and miracles from God and the Universe.

Another form of Earth out of balance, is when you have more than enough of what you need to survive but are afraid that you will lose it all. Out of control hoarding or being miserly and holding onto money and material possessions out of fear that you'll never have more, are evidence of an unhealthy Earth elemental force.

**Mineral Healthy and Balanced:** You know your Mineral elemental force is switched on when you have the experience of living on purpose, along with clarity for living your truth, and curiosity and excitement about life. Healthy Mineral is like being on top of the mountain and clearly seeing the bigger picture of your life and your world. In this state, you seek and welcome healthy connections to people, situations and opportunities that will support you in the fulfillment of your dreams and happy endings. You are eager to learn new things, as well as share your personal stories and wisdom. People who choose to do their *wisdom walk* or seek out any form of guidance to support their conscious personal growth, are people with healthy Mineral.

**Your Unhealthy Mineral:** When Mineral is overwhelming and out of balance, it's like being shut up in a room full of treasures but from which you can't escape. In other words, you mind goes on overload. In this state, severe mental illnesses can appear along with anti-social and reclusive behavior. Throughout history, there are cases of people who have demonstrated their genius and then go insane. The painter, Vincent Van Gogh, is a famous example of out-of-balance Mineral.

Your Mineral in the switched-off position can also appear as loss of memory, amnesia, or even Alzheimer's disease. A low frequency Mineral force can show up as a person who is insecure about their self-worth and uses their accumulation of knowledge to prove that they are better than others. In this state, you relate to others through anti-social behaviors such as stubbornness, arrogance, superiority complex, bigotry, racism, sexism, religious fundamentalism, and delusions of grandeur. People who think they don't need to grow and heal themselves, are people with unhealthy Mineral.

**Nature Healthy and Balanced:** The best way to understand your healthy Nature is to think of childhood innocence. Think about the way in which children are naturally open to learning and doing new things. Think about how excited they can be about growing an inch or turning another year older. They welcome the natural changes of their life. As an adult in a state of healthy Nature, you embrace the journey of life and look forward to becoming the best version of yourself through personal growth and development. You are able to trust and go with the flow of life. You have no fear of death because you have no fear of life. You are able to be authentic, natural, and unique, walking your own life path with courage and gratitude. You believe in everyday magic and allow your imagination and creativity to lead you to your dreams come true. When your Nature elemental essence is switched on, you know that you are an essential part of the Universe's grand design. You believe that you have value and that you matter.

**Your Unhealthy Nature:** Living in *Never-Never Land*, the home of Peter Pan, the boy who never wanted to grow up, is the best way to understand Nature out of balance. Unhealthy Nature is about fear of and resistance to change. In this state, you are afraid of dying because you afraid of living. You attempt to passively control others by using self-pity, self-sabotage, or aloofness. You choose to stay stuck in your past story of pain. You may stay in relationships, jobs, or living environments long after they've stopped working for you. You spend more time playing roles in order to please others, rather than focusing on your truth and learning to please yourself.

Unhealthy Nature can also swing the other way and show up as someone who is unable to make commitments or be truthful in relationships. Manipulation, lying, betrayal and aggressive controlling behaviors like intimidation, characterize someone whose Nature is out of balance. These are the persons who demonstrate a lack of reverence for life and humanity. You become so stuck in your own negativity that you are unable to be considerate of anyone or anything else.

So, now that you have some of the basics about the contents of the Dagara Medicine Wheel, in the next chapter I will share about the healing power of this cosmogony and the five eternal truths that it has spoken to me.

# Chapter 9

# The Healing Power of the Dagara Medicine Wheel

## *Beyond Our Intellect*

*T*he process of healing emotional pain requires something that goes way beyond our intellectual knowing. Authentic healing requires more than our ability to reason, to analyze, and think rationally. I'm not talking about healing as covering up pain, or convincing yourself that you just have to grin, bear it, and get used to living with it for the rest of your life. I'm talking about eliminating the suffering and misery you feel when you're all alone, and before you get the chance to unconsciously or consciously transfer that pain onto everyone and everything around you! Transforming emotional pain means eliminating it, and THIS IS NOT AN INTELLECTUAL EXERCISE!

The Dagara Medicine Wheel contains a power within it to heal and transform emotional pain because it can bypass our intellect. The Dagara Medicine Wheel has the spiritual power to connect us to our Soul. It came into being at a time when humans had to believe in their direct connection to the Earth, to the animals, the stars, to their gods, the Universe, and to each other. This belief in unity consciousness is what enabled them to emotionally and physically survive in a world without the modern conveniences we take for granted. Our ancient ancestors had to believe in their Soul power to overcome trouble, pain, and the natural obstacles to living in harmony, peace, and love. Otherwise, none of us would be alive today.

In this post-modern world we live in, it is very challenging to believe that a Greater Order and Direction, a mysterious, unknowable force really has our back. We doubt that the mystery we call "God" is always in support of our healing and evolution. We've learned to read and write and question even that which is unknowable. That rational "seeing is believing" part of our mind will do whatever it can to block us from fully engaging with the healing power of God, the Universe, the Great Mystery. It is only by connecting to our Soul that we are more able to access the unbounded knowledge and love from something much greater than what our human brain can fully grasp.

When emotional pain shows up, to avoid dealing with it, our intellect will tell us stuff like this:

> *There's no reason for you to be in pain. That mess happened 20 years ago. You should be over that by now!*

> *This pain ain't real because you read that self-help book, you attended that weekend workshop, you paid for the on-line spiritual class, and you've already cried about this mess 100 times!*

> *Why is this pain coming up now? You don't have time for this! Pull yourself together, man-up, and don't let the pain win!*

> *Just ignore it and it will go away.*

Your intellect, your rational mind, and let's not leave out your fear, will always try to block you from being connected to your soul. That's what they do. However, unless you have a soul-connection (also called your love-connection), you will not be able to truthfully acknowledge, accept, feel, and release your emotional pain.

Pain must be recognized, acknowledged and released

before it can be transformed. Now let's be clear, you have to be conscious of the truth of who you are at the soul level in order to choose to let go of, and eliminate, your suffering and misery. This is why the Dagara Medicine Wheel is such a powerful ancient, sacred treasure. Whether you see a picture of it, hear about the creation story it carries, feel a resonance with the element you were born through, or open up to learning about more ways to access its medicine, this wisdom from West Africa is automatically connecting you to your Soul.

## The Voice of the Dagara Medicine Wheel

In the opening scenes of the movie, *2001: A Space Odyssey (1968)*, the audience is introduced to a mysterious black monolith, a large single upright block of stone. Although no one in the movie ever explains to the audience what the monolith is, where it came from, or why it came, you as a viewer understand that it is something beyond human intellect. What you do know is that every time that monolith shows up things evolve! (Of course the filmmaker's brilliant use of the fanfare called "Sunrise" from Richard Strauss's 19th century New Age music, *Also Sprach Zarathustra*, really helps!)

The black monolith clearly possesses an energy that enables those who see or touch it to have a transcendent experience. They gain a greater knowing, a higher consciousness than what they had before. This describes my experience with the Dagara Medicine Wheel. It possesses a power that supports transformation of emotional pain like nothing else I've ever experienced. I always feel moved to a higher place in my psyche when I work with this sacred tool.

Now let's face it, no one in their right mind wants to have to acknowledge, accept, and feel their emotional pain in order to release it and have it transformed. Especially not that pain that is connected to things from your childhood, or the plight of your ancestors. As I stated before, pain cannot be transformed unless you are willing and able to let it go. The letting go process can be so challenging and frightening that most people choose to stay stuck in their pain. *You know who I'm talking about!* They wear it like a badge of honor, attracting people into their life to dump it onto. (Yes! I did that too at one point!) It is because of this resistance in humans to healing and growth that I believe the Dagara Medicine Wheel, with its ancient wisdom of the five primal elements, is so important in the world today.

During the now 18 years that I have been blessed to know, personally work with, and teach about this precious gift from Africa, I've come to learn that the Dagara Medicine Wheel has a very strong voice. It's not a voice that you can hear with the hearing that is part of your five senses. This type of hearing is not imaginary or delusional either. It is what you experience with your "third ear", which lives in your heart and soul. The wheel speaks to me of faith, hope, courage, confidence, validation, joy, happiness, harmony, peace, and love.

The Dagara Medicine Wheel has also spoken to me of what I call *eternal truths.* Eternal truths come from a Greater Order and Direction, are beyond the intelligence of humans, and can therefore *never not be true.* These truths will always exist as long as humans exists. This is wonderful treasure. It is the treasure of the eternal truth of who you are as a human being. In a world where skin color, educational background, language, and even the condition of teeth can create judgement and separation among people, it is vital to know that your true Self is way beyond those temporal things.

The eternal truths that the Dagara Medicine Wheel speaks to my heart and soul are: **(1)** *you were born full,* **(2)** *you are enough,* **(3)** *you have a divine purpose,* **(4)** *your soul can heal the world,* **and (5)** *you are not disposable.*

# Eternal Truth #1: You Were Born Full

Being born full means that the truth of who you are is imbedded in your bones. Because human beings possess a skeletal system, we are born with a library of information, ideas, thoughts, dreams, and feelings that are older than time itself. Everything we need to know in order to live healthily, happily, and on purpose, is encoded in our bones. Modern scientists call this our DNA. We are born full, and it is the job of parents and all adults in a community to help children remember, versus learn, the truth of who they are and why they exist. Being born full you have genius. You have a purpose in life. You are connected to everything in the universe. You have the ability to make a difference in the world, and experience fulfillment, or "Happy Endings," in life.

# Eternal Truth #2: You Are Enough

Every human being possesses the spark of the Divine. The word 'divine' comes from the Latin word "*divus*", which means "*of a god*". So you and every human on the planet are divine. The truth of who you are as a divine being is so much more powerful than being financially and materially successful. You are unique, as is everyone else around you. Whatever happens to you, happens for a divine reason. Don't waste time comparing yourself, your situation, or your life to that of others. You will only and always measure up less than them. Embrace who you are as whole and complete. You are walking the path of life in order to remember how fantastic and uniquely magnificent you truly are. Accept and love yourself unconditionally.

# Eternal Truth #3: You Have a Divine Purpose

Before you took possession of your body, your soul made promises about what you would accomplish during your Earthly walk. Your mind would go crazy if you knew consciously at birth exactly how to keep those promises. So, a developmental process was created uniquely for you. As you move through life, you are given greater order and direction about your higher purpose at the right time, and in the right way. Often you may judge a situation that comes to you as trouble, but along with trouble comes treasure. Look for it. Expect it. Ask for it to be revealed. Being on purpose is messy, but the rewards are sensational.

# Eternal Truth #4: Your Soul Can Heal the World

Your soul is not your personality. Your soul was never born and can never die. Your soul is the best part of being human because it never judges you, shames you, blames you, or abandons you. It loves you unconditionally and encourages you to share that love with everyone and everything around you. Connecting with your soul is choosing Love over Fear, because your soul doesn't know or engage with fear. When fear shows up, your connection to your soul disappears. When you call forth your courage, you are calling upon your soul. When you call out to it, you get reconnected and your fears vanish. Moving away from Fear and returning to Love is what healing is truly all about. If everyone in the world would consciously connect to their soul on a daily basis, then the world would be healed.

# Eternal Truth #5: You Are Not Disposable

There are no disposable humans. The Dagara creation story shows how all five elements must co-exist and work together in order for there to be life. The elemental portals of the medicine wheel teach how unique and essential each elemental being is to life on our planet. Fire isn't better than Water. They are two very different elemental energies that came together to birth the Earth. Earth isn't better or more important than Fire or Water. It's just different. But without these three primary elements, there would be no plants, no animals, and no us!

There is no natural need for racism, sexism, classism, or any form of hierarchy and divisiveness. These are human constructs, or inventions, that are fear-based and destructive to peace, harmony, and fulfillment in life. The history of separation, exclusion, and oppression among humans is very long, and very tragic. The deeply rooted belief that certain people, and groups of people, are disposable is alive and kicking in the post-modern, technologically advanced era.

It is hard to believe that after the horrors of Trans-Atlantic slavery, American Indian genocide, the Jewish Holocaust during World War II, and the dropping of two atomic bombs on Japanese citizens, that humans are still not willing and able to have reverence for human life. To human detriment, mass murder occurs in schools and public places once thought to be safe, nuclear power plants are built in earthquake zones, and every week there is an unlawful killing of Black men by fear-filled law enforcers. The belief in disposable people exists all over the world. We see it where ever there is war, and threats of war. Shifting out of such a deeply embedded belief system, that is virtually unconscious for most humans, will take an enormous amount of effort. It all begins with making a choice to believe that humans are not disposable and that they are Divine.

## In Conclusion

I believe this ancient tool called the Dagara Medicine Wheel gives us great hope. It is a powerful tool that can aid us as we work to shift human consciousness from being lorded over by fear to the generating and sharing of love. Imagine if every child born were treated by their family and community members as if their existence was essential to the well-being of their family, community, and the world. Imagine that instead of having to compare themselves with others, children would learn that they are unique and valuable — exactly the way they are, which Mr. Rogers told children through his television show every day! What if elemental purpose and inherent gifts were more important for a healthy and harmonious life than getting a Ph.D., having a million-dollar bank account, or the "right" body type? Imagine that!

# Chapter 10

# Stories of Pain Transformed

## Introduction

*I* n the previous chapter, I talked about what I've experienced as the five (5) eternal truths of the Dagara Medicine Wheel, which are:

1. *You were born full.*
2. *You are enough*
3. *You have a Divine purpose.*
4. *Your soul can heal the world.*
5. *You are not disposable, you are Divine.*

In this chapter, I will share stories from four of the men who participated in and graduated from the *Wisdom Walk to Self-Mastery* program.

Each of these men suffered severe trauma and adverse experiences in childhood that was never fully addressed. They all have perpetrated or threatened violence against an intimate partner. Three of them had been cycling through the prison system before coming to the program. All of them are highly intelligent, but this was not reflected in their academic history. For most of them, the dysfunctional conditions of home and their neighborhood often disrupted their school attendance.

Despite and probably because of their backgrounds, each of these men whole-heartedly participated in the healing practices and rituals of the Dagara Medicine Wheel. I'm so honored to have been given permission by these four men to share their stories of personal transformation with you. It is their intent and hope that you will be inspired and strengthened on your own journey towards your happy endings and fulfillment in life.

## Max's Story

During my recruitment process for my first cohort for the *Wisdom Walk to Self-Mastery* program, I was asked to interview a man at a half-way house. It was a community-based, low-security facility used to help men re-enter more effectively from prison. It was at this neighborhood detention facility that I met Max. I made a habit of never reading the criminal backgrounds of the men I was recruiting until they completed the program. I never wanted to be biased or judgmental about their ability to engage in the deep dive of the *Wisdom Walk* program. That practice really paid off regarding my experience with Max.

Max was born into a third-generation immigrant family from Poland. His parents were hardworking, law-abiding citizens, living the typical Midwestern, middle class lifestyle. Max was highly intelligent as a child, but he told me that he became the target of his father's pain body. I had the unusual opportunity to meet and talk with Max's father. He told me that he took full responsibility for his son's violent behavior, which had Max cycling through the criminal justice system.

During my initial meeting with Max, I gave him an overview of the program, which included my use of cinema to support my teachings. He shared with me that he liked to read the book that a film was based upon before watching the movie, so that he could do a comparison. At the time, he was in the process of reading *There Will Be Blood*, a film that had been recently released about the Texas oil battles. I thought to myself, "Good, he's open to learning." But, after I finished my spiel, he said he didn't want to do the program because he'd been through so many before. He also knew the majority of men attending would be Black, and that wasn't feeling too good to him.

When I left the facility, I breathed a sigh of relief. The last thing I wanted in my program was a bigoted sociopath who had the word 'assassin' written all over him. The following week though, I received a call from Max. I hadn't left him any contact information, so I was very surprised that he was able to remember the name of my organization. He also remembered my name and pronounced it correctly. He asked if he could join the cohort. He said that he changed his mind because he had never tried the spiritual stuff before. I knew that taking him on would be a huge risk, but I also knew that if he got out of line, he would go back to prison. So, I let go of my fears and said, yes.

Max responded surprisingly and immediately well to all aspects of the program. He demonstrated appreciation for all the new and different information to which he was being exposed. He had no problem participating as the only White male in the group. Of course, he also liked being let out of detention three times a week to come to class, be he genuinely liked the class and helped with the setting up and cleaning up afterwards.

I think the most important piece in the learning experience for Max was that I acknowledged his intelligence. He especially loved the movie time. He loved talking about the themes and the music of the films, and always analyzed how the storylines and characters connected to the healing process. He would lay out on the carpet of the room we used, eating his popcorn, and being totally engrossed.

Max's element is Water, and hearing that his nature was peacemaking really touched something deep in his soul. I'll never forget the awakened look on his face the day I shared the wisdom of the Dagara Medicine Wheel. It was like he could finally remember his truth and not pretend anymore.

During our work on ancestral wounds, Max was able to

bring in an original vintage photo of his great-great uncle, who amazingly looked like his twin. This uncle was the 'black sheep' of the family. His criminal behavior was the reason for leaving his homeland of Poland. The family set him up in a house on the same street but avoided him like the plague. The ancestor altar is an essential fixture in the environment of the program, so Max placed the picture of his uncle on it and opened himself up to receiving non-physical guidance and help. We asked the look-a-like ancestor to help Max break the cycle of crime and violence within the family.

A huge turning point occurred for Max shortly after that. By week-five of this intensive 12-week process, he found it really hard not to tell the truth. He had stolen something from another detainee's room, and when confronted he confessed and was scheduled to be sent back to jail. With tears in his eyes, Max shared his story with me and asked if he could return to complete the program. I assured him that he could.

About six months later, at the request of his parents, I visited Max in the downtown jail right before his release. He shared with me how he was really done with going to prison, and I again assured him that he could return to the program. By the time Max graduated from the *Wisdom Walk*, he had demonstrated his belief in his true nature. He was living respectfully and peacefully with his parents, lovingly tending their flower garden. He avoided using cocaine. He sought forgiveness from a woman he had stalked and threatened. He reached out to his children. He secured a transitional job as a waiter with a prominent catering company. He also got into a new relationship and told his partner all about his criminal background. Calling me his stepmom, he brought the young woman to my office for me to meet and get my approval. I was humbled and grateful.

Today, Max lives independently and is steadily working as a highly trained technician manufacturing machine parts. He continues to work on his addictive behaviors, but he's never gone back to his former lifestyle. He is remaining true to his Water nature.

## Adam's Story

Adam was raised in a middle class, Midwestern environment by a single mom after she and his father divorced. As a young child, Adam and his siblings would spend most of their summers with their father and stepmom. It was during this time period that Adam was sexually abused. The abuse happened for several years before the truth came out.

Like most survivors of sexual abuse, Adam had no idea how his embedded trauma would bring so much struggling and suffering into his adolescent and young adult life. At the time of his participation in the *Wisdom Walk* program, Adam was unemployed and having disruptive post-traumatic stress symptoms. He self-medicated with a daily routine of smoking several packs of Marlboro cigarettes, and drinking lots of Mountain Dew soda. He was not allowed to visit with his two young children.

Adam showed up for his recruitment interview dressed in black, wearing black finger nail polish and being very suspicious of me and the program. When I asked about his religious and/or spiritual beliefs he informed me that he was an atheist. I told him that wasn't a problem because he didn't need to believe in anything but himself for the spirit medicine to do its work on him. Clearly, Adam had a willingness to learn something new and was open to heal his emotional pain from the past. So, he decided to give the program and me a chance.

Adam is a Mineral person and he really appreciated the opportunity to discuss and honor the ancestors. He was part of the third generation of Austrian and German immigrants and he had done much research into the family history. He brought in hard and digital copies of vintage ancestor pictures and shared a few stories. When he learned how we can connect with the ancestors for support in healing the family wounds that got transferred from one generation to the next, his time and energy into researching them made really good sense.

The Fire Ritual is the initial experience of community healing for *Wisdom Walk* participants. For most of the men, this is when they begin to experience a huge shift in their psyche and ultimately their lives. Adam was very skeptical about the ritual work. He couldn't bend his rational mind to believe that making a faith gesture with a group of men and a weird Black shaman woman could do anything to impact how he was feeling about himself and his life. I reassured him that he didn't need to adopt any belief in any god in order to benefit from the process. All he needed to do was be willing to experience something new in his life, including an end to his suffering.

It was shortly after the Fire Ritual that things began to quickly change for Adam. He became more awake to how he was drifting through life and realized that he had a choice to not be a victim to his past. He realized he wanted to be a father to his children and began to seriously take steps to be able to have visits with them. He had a passion for computer animation and also began to talk seriously about going to a school to get certified in his skills.

At the *Wisdom Walk* graduation, which we call the Presentations of Learning or POLs, I'll never forget what Adam shared with the audience: "I don't know what Jojopah does or understand what all this stuff is about. I just know that it works!" In the words of Adam's aunt who expressed her gratitude to me for the program, "The changes I've witnessed in my nephew are mind-blowing."

Today, Adam continues to choose not to be a victim to his past or life in general. Not only did he go to school and graduate, but he was asked to become part of the faculty and teach. Currently, he has stepped into being an entrepreneur and an administrator as he and a group of colleagues are establishing a school of their own. He continues to be a positive and loving father to his children. He is now in a new and stable relationship, and he and his partner recently had a baby together. Of course since graduating from *Wisdom Walk* he's faced many challenges, emotional, social and financial. Yet, he's never let go of choosing to live his life on purpose.

## Jason's Story

I first met Jason when he participated in the *Wisdom Walk* program that was part of a pioneering prison re-entry project that we called, *Alma House*. Jason was one of the first residents who would live in a 16-bed facility for at least three months to receive information, guidance and support before returning to community life. Up until that time, Jason had been in prison for many years. Much of that had been in solitary confinement along with the use of prescribed neurological drugs. Like most of the men coming directly from prison to a low-security residence in an under-resourced neighborhood, there was a challenging emotional and social period of adjustment. Along with all of the innovative methodologies that created the healing-focused culture of the Alma House, the *Wisdom Walk* provided Jason with much needed opportunities to deeply connect to his soul.

At the beginning of every class, I would clear the men's negative energy using the smoke of burning white sage. This is an ancient custom of many Native tribes of North America. Jason was surprised and grateful to be able to connect with his ancient roots in this manner. He eventually performed the sage ceremony for the class. He also really appreciated the presence of an ancestor altar. He shared some pictures of his ancestors and generously shared sacred items that are still part of the altar to this day. The *Wisdom Walk to Self-Mastery* program, with its inclusion of indigenous spirituality, sparked a remembrance within Jason of values and principles that he'd been exposed to growing up.

Jason jumped into his healing journey with both feet, determined to reinvent his life. He took full advantage of all the Alma House services and even joined a Native healing circle in his community. He weaned himself off of the prescription drugs and adopted a stray cat of whom he took extremely good care. By the time he left the Alma House, Jason had a job and soon after had his own apartment. There were challenges along the way, but Jason never gave up on himself or his commitment to become the best version of himself.

Today, Jason is happily married and living in a rural area in the South. He is steadily employed, grows organic vegetables, and stays very connected to people and events that honor his Native heritage. Miraculously, although Jason knows the heartache and hurdles he had to jump over, he has been reunited with his youngest son. They've even gone to the Grand Canyon together, and Jason is continuously learning how to be the best father for his son. Jason is an excellent writer, and always is willing to respond to a request to publicly share his personal story of healing and transformation. I expect to be reading his book in the near future. Ahau! (Native expression for *right on!*)

## Floyd's Story

Floyd and his siblings grew up in the two most infamous Chicago public housing projects, Cabrini-Green and Robert Taylor Homes, which were demolished over a 15-year period from 1995 to 2010. Both of his parents are Black Americans who migrated north from the deep south to find more job opportunities and a better way of life. Unfortunately, their beginning experience in the Midwest was traumatizing and horrendous for them and their children.

Cabrini-Green and the Robert Taylor Homes, were very close to downtown Chicago and surrounded by wealthy neighborhoods. These projects became controlled by drug lords who operated a billion-dollar enterprise, linked to Columbian and other drug cartels within both Central and South America. Strangely enough, Cabrini-Green, whose namesake was a Catholic nun known for her undying service to impoverished immigrants, was built on cursed grounds, formerly known as "Little Hell". In the late 1860s it was the site of Chicago's first slums and gangster infested neighborhoods for the Irish and Italian Mafias.

The first of Chicago's public housing project was constructed from 1942-45. It was created as the way to clean up the rampant crime and dilapidated housing of "Little Hell." Originally, the resident population was predominantly European Americans. But when Black workers were the first to be laid off from the war-related factory jobs that had lured them to Chicago, the city built 15 high-rise units between 1955-57 to address the growing need for low-income urban housing. By the 1980s, Cabrini-Green, Robert Taylor Homes and the other nearby housing projects had been neglected and abandoned by the city government and the police. Both children and adults were exposed to relentless drug crime with deadly gang wars and the daily threats of stray bullets. Even the Emergency Medical professionals avoided responding to 911 calls from these projects. Within the units themselves, there was deteriorating infrastructure of every kind from lighting, plumbing and elevators, as well as the infestation of roaches and rats.

Floyd's early childhood with his mother and father was normal to him. He played with his siblings and friends and followed the safety rules taught to them by his parents. But sadly, Floyd's father became trapped in the hell of drug addiction. One afternoon he didn't come home at the usual time that Floyd expected. With the loss of his father, the projects became a true nightmare for the family. He witnessed traumatic things to which no human should ever be exposed. When the family moved north from Chicago, initially the new low-income neighborhood in Milwaukee was like paradise compared to where they'd been living. Tragically, the most severe experiences of trauma awaited Floyd, from a domestically violent home, a sexually abusive nurse at a hospital, and his teenage drug dealing which unsurprisingly landed him in prison.

Floyd's commitment to reinvent his life started in a jail cell. He'd already served several years in prison but had new charges brought against him while on probation. He was now a father, and his son was still a toddler. He didn't want to repeat what his father had done with him, so he prayed to God and asked to be spared a return to prison. Miraculously, his charges at the time were dropped, and he was put back on probation.

Floyd was court-ordered to the Alma Center's *Men Ending Violence* program for six months. His quick learning, positive attitude, and natural leadership ability impressed the facilitators. They referred him to the *Wisdom Walk* program believing that a deeper dive into his healing would be very beneficial. Floyd had no intentions of staying around for another three months, but he trusted the facilitators.

When I did my recruitment interview with Floyd, like most of the men, he was surprised to see a Black woman dressed in an African robe and head wrap, with a candle-lit altar of stones and strange objects in her office. As I told him about his elemental essence, which is Nature, he was totally blown away. Neither of us knew at that time that he would become a facilitator and the next steward of the program.

From the first day of the program, Floyd connected to the African spirituality and indigenous healing modalities with ease and effortlessness. He never missed a class, often coming early to help with set up, and remaining to help with clean up.

After the first ritual, which was Fire, Floyd experienced a huge shift in his belief system. He had a barbecue with family and friends, and it was just laughter, good food, and fun. There was no disruptive melodrama or violence. This experience became his proof that he could reinvent his life.

After Floyd graduated, he chose to return and experience the program again. In his second go-round he demonstrated an adept ability to inspire and encourage the other men. By the time he did his third *Wisdom Walk*, I asked him to be a volunteer peer mentor. In addition to supporting the men during class, he made himself available in the evening when the temptation level was turned all the way up. He was able to talk several men out of becoming violent with their partners, as well as coaching one man out of shooting someone. All through-out his work with the men, Floyd continued to work on himself.

Currently, after five years of apprenticeship as both a peer mentor and a co-facilitator, Floyd serves as the lead facilitator and steward of the *Wisdom Walk to Self-Mastery* program. He is now an essential full-time staff member of the Alma Center. He has brought his own experiences, wisdom and creativity to the work, and is more inspirational and directive for the men than I could ever be. Floyd has a very close and loving relationship with his son and has even reconciled with his father. As a gifted public speaker who never refuses a request to tell his personal story, Floyd has brought attention to the Alma Center that has manifested supporters and funding from local and state government, as well as private foundations. Most recently, Floyd received recognition for his incredible contribution of healing for the men of his community, from *The Mankind Project*, a national peer training group whose mission is to initiate and support the emotional wellness of men.

# Part Three

# UNDERSTANDING AND PREPARING FOR THE HEALING JOURNEY

# Chapter 11

## Asking for Help

### Let's Start from the Very Beginning

*P*reparation is always required to make a safe and successful journey. In these next five chapters, I'm going to share information and tools that all wisdom walkers can use to support their individual, unique, and collective healing process. I've included the word 'collective" here because ancient wisdom teaches that when one of us experiences a healing, the energy impacts all of us. We are all energetically connected, so your healing journey is never just about you. It touches and helps everyone around you. When one of us gets free, we all get freed!

The beginning of any journey is truly a powerful time. You say goodbye to home and all that is familiar. Even though you may have a destination, the getting there is a big unknown. You must have the courage to take on a big risk. The same is true for the Wisdom Walk journey. The home you are leaving for this healing journey is the level of consciousness out of which you presently operate. Your current level of consciousness is filled with what you believe is true, or not true, about yourself and the world around you. If your *pain body* has been running and ruining your life, and/or taking you through the same dramas and upsets over and over and over again, then your current level of consciousness is not enough for you. It's not enough to get you to a life of joy, happiness, loving support, fulfillment, or happy endings. The Wisdom Walk, as a journey through your internal landscape, will provide information and experiences needed to grow your consciousness. This expansion of your consciousness will automatically grow your personal beliefs about who and what you are.

Moving up from one level of consciousness to another is how you gain the power and strength to transform your emotional pain into pure Love, for your Self and others. As I've stated previously, this is not just an intellectual exercise or rational process. You can't think your way up to a higher consciousness. You need help, and not just from other humans. You need help from a Great Order and Direction, a Higher Intelligence, the Galactic Center of the Universe, your Ancestors, or whatever name you want to call it. The need for this non-physical and supernal help is why the Wisdom Walk is a sacred journey.

## Accepting Your Mess

Asking for help at the very beginning of the Wisdom Walk journey is how you can acknowledge to your Self that you are willing to engage in a sacred process. This doesn't mean that asking for help isn't hard, because it is! What makes the asking so hard is that by asking, you are admitting that you are in need of help. You are admitting to yourself that something is not right, something is out-of-balance, something is wrong on your insides. When you ask for help it means you are not at peace with yourself, despite the many excuses you may have made in denial, and how much you may have been blaming everyone around you. In addition, your pain body and the trauma-related thoughts it creates (*trauma mind*), may be working overtime to keep you in denial through some form of addiction. Whether it's drugs, sex, gambling, over-shopping, over-working, over-eating, or daily Netflix and Hulu bingeing, that hurting part of yourself will make it very challenging for you to accept your internal mess.

Unless you are willing and able to accept the messy

disturbance from within, you can't do anything to change or transform your pain. It is for this important reason, that taking time to first ask for help is the true start for the Wisdom Walk journey. The way in which you ask for help needs to be done in a sacred manner. What I mean is, you create a right and respectful environment, you get still, and you humble yourself to a Great Order and Direction.

Right and respectful environment means being some place quiet and safe where you can't be distracted. Your asking for help requires your full attention. Getting still is not just what you do physically, it also means quieting your mind. Remember, your pain body and the trauma mind (*Thing 1 and Thing 2*) will work over time to sabotage your healing. You can't let your pain body convince you that what you're doing won't work, or that you don't deserve it to work! When it tries to discourage you with negative thoughts and accusations, tell it this, *"That may be true, but I'm open to learning something new!"*

You see, you don't have to have your journey all figured out for it to be successful. You just need to be willing to go on the journey. I believe it's comforting to know that our willingness is all that is needed to step onto the path of healing. The journey will reveal itself as we just put one foot in front of the other. Humbling oneself to a greater and invisible power means making the ask from a belief that God, the Universe, or whatever you claim as a Higher Intelligence, not only knows more than you, but that it knows and is designed to deliver what's best for your healing. When you humble yourself in this manner, you are not thinking of or treating yourself as less. You are wisely proclaiming your belief that the world is out to gift you. And so, it will.

Previously, in Chapter 5, I talked about surrender as a form of communication with all the loving entities of the Cosmos who are guiding your every step toward fulfillment and "happy endings." That deep surrender is the same as asking for help for your healing journey. A very simple yet powerful way to ask for help is this:

*God/Universe/Higher Self, I ask and thank you for my healing journey.*

*Help me, Help me, Help me!*

*I receive, I receive, I receive. Ashé! (And so, it is.)*

## Starting Off Cleanly

In addition to being willing to ask for the help you will need for your sacred journey, it is necessary to have what I call a clean relationship with your God as you begin the Wisdom Walk. By "clean" I mean you don't set co-dependent, one-way bargains. For example, *"God, if you help me get my healing, I will go back to church; quit drinking and smoking; stop cursing; etc."* The reason that you don't want to go this route is because your healing is already promised. You don't have to bargain for it. The only reason you wouldn't experience your healing is because you choose not to. As I mentioned previously, healing is a choice.

The other important reason why bargaining with your Greater Order and Direction is not necessary is because of the evolutionary impulse of the Universe. Thanks to the Hubble Telescope, the Voyager Probe, and the Kepler Space Observatory, which has found over 1000 new planets, science has visual proof of how the Universe works. We can visually understand that the Universe is all about life and death and evolution. We now have unearthly photos of the magnificent dust and gas clouds where stars are born, and mind-blowing pictures of the remaining material from the explosions of dying stars. We also now know that we are part of a huge galaxy, full of billions of stars and planets, even more than we can count. As inhabitants of this Universe, it is safe to say that we are also part of an evolutionary impulse. In light of all this wondrous new scientific information, I think it's safe to say that being called or moved to a process of healing and growth is quite natural and normal. You just have to believe that there is a force within you that knows how to heal your internal mess.

As you cleanly begin the Wisdom Walk journey, not making any bargains, you establish a higher relationship with your Divine Self. This is the part of you that is your soul. Connecting to your soul is essential. With soul connection you will be more able to continue to ask for help as you move forward along the journey. You will be more able to experience blessings without feeling guilty or unworthy. You will be more able to walk in faith and not get easily discouraged. You will know that you can make the choice for healing and growth. Ashé!

# Chapter 12

# Setting Your Healing Goals

*L* ike any journey, a healing journey comes with challenges. There will be times when you question why you are doing it. There will be times when you want to turn back or feel like you can't go any farther. The reality of doubt and fear coming to knock makes the setting of your healing goals essential for your Wisdom Walk. The goals must be beacons of light for you when you're in the dark parts of your journey. They must clearly and deeply remind you of what is waiting for you. They must provide you with steadfast hope and unwavering encouragement. So, here is a guide to support you with identifying your healing goals. This guide goes beyond, *I want to be out of pain,* and into the heart of the matter, in which your pain is rooted.

## STEP 1: *Visions and Dreams*

The emotional pain and imbalance that you are seeking to heal is blocking you from doing, having and/or being something more in your life. By first stating your vision and dreams for yourself, you are giving yourself the true reasons for stepping into a healing process. It's always a good idea to make your thought process sacred. The simplest way to do this is to begin with a prayer. Taking a moment to get still and communicate with a Greater Order and Direction is always beneficial. You can keep it simple by saying something like this:

*God, Higher Self, Ancestors, push my fear aside and give me access to my truth. Thank you, thank you, thank you! Amen/Ashé/And so it is!*

Next, write down your truest and most heart-felt answers to the following questions:

1. What do you want to do in your life to be loved and loving?
2. What do you want to have in your life, so you can feel proud and peaceful?
3. What do you want to be for your Self and others, so you have no shame or regrets?

## STEP 2: Inspirational Statement of Goals

Once you have answered all three questions and you feel good about your answers, you put them into a statement that becomes your light and reminder along the Wisdom Walk journey. Here's an example of what I'm talking about, using the following answers to the 3 questions above:

*I am taking this Wisdom Walk healing journey so that I can stop living in fear, have a job where I am appreciated and paid well, and become forgiving of people who hurt me in the past, as well as receive forgiveness for those I have hurt.*

## STEP 3: Posting Reminders

Once you are completely satisfied with your statement – and you'll know this because it will put a smile on your face, post it somewhere that you can easily see it and be reminded. A bathroom and/or bedroom mirror works well!

During your journey as you experience your transformation, your healing goals may also expand. You may also identify one or two more goals you'd like to achieve. This is a very natural and validating part of any growth process. What's most important is that you know you have set personal intentions that have meaning for you. Your healing goals will help to guide you along the path and enable you to outlast any thoughts of doubt fear, unworthiness, or defeat. They will help you sustain your courage and commitment to putting your pain body under new management –which is your Higher Self!

Below is an example of the Community Healing Goals that were set by a cohort of men in the *Wisdom Walk* program at the Alma Center. This communal list of goals was created from each community member's individual healing goal. I only organized their similar goals and named the themes:

*During Our Wisdom Walk (Winter/Spring 2011), we intend to heal and grow by addressing the following issues:*

1. **Co-dependency**: I choose to no longer be a slave to the emotional pain of others. I choose inter-dependence, to take full responsibility for my own emotional well-being and learn to transform versus transfer my pain.

2. **Authenticity** versus People Pleasing: I choose to no longer participate in people pleasing and false obligation in order to be able to love myself and have others love me. I choose instead to learn how to love my Self unconditionally and to believe that I am enough. (Self-sufficiency)

3. **Self-cleansing**: I choose to release the belief that I am dirty, damaged and defeated. I now choose to completely trust my own internal healing power because I am in the Universe and the Universe is within me. I choose to believe that the Universe is designed to be generative

and not destructive as it moves through a continuous, never-ending cycle of death and rebirth.

4. **Mama Drama**: I choose to release my attachment to my mother's core wound and my ancestral wounds, and the shame, blame, judgment, depression and violence that it can create in my life. I choose to recreate and support my Self as normal, capable, belonging, loving, and loved.

5. **Daddy Drama**: I choose to release my attachment to the core wound of my father, and his father, and all of my male ancestors. I choose instead to walk my own path, unfettered by the past, and supported by my own internal truth and divine guidance about authentic manhood, husbandry, and fatherhood.

6. **Abandonment**: I choose to forgive all those who abandoned me as I grew from a child into a man. I no longer believe it was my fault. I now choose to learn how never to abandon my Self by strengthening my connection to my Higher Self daily. In this way I will not abandon my children and loved ones ever again.

7. **Vacant Self Esteem**: I choose to remember, refine and share my unique gifts and talents with my family, friends, community, and my Self. I no longer choose to compare myself to others because I will always end up as less than. I choose to believe that I am a unique and loving human who was created for an important purpose that will enhance all of humanity.

# Chapter 13

# Being Willing Not to Know

## Being Conditioned to Having All The Answers

*W*hen I was in elementary school, during the early 1960s, my classmates and I sat at brown wooden desks that were nailed to the floor, in perfect rows, one right behind the other. I remember the remnants of an ink well on each desk, which by then were just holes at the top and to the right, with tarnished brass covers over them that you could lift up and down. In this formation of seating, you couldn't turn your seat or desk around to learn in teams. You had to stay in your place. It was designed for you to look to the front of the room at the teacher and the blackboard.

In this very structured environment, learning was all about *having to know*. The worst experience for any student was to have the teacher call on you to respond to a question, and you not have the correct answer. So, for me and my elementary school mates, to avoid the embarrassment of not knowing the correct answer, we spent most of our time memorizing information. There was no opportunity to learn about things that really interested us. Also, there was no consideration of what things were more aligned with our individual and particular learning styles.

My elementary class of about fifteen students, at Public School (PS) 40 on Staten Island in New York City, was considered one of the smartest groups of children in the history of the school. I remember being told by our 1st grade teacher, Mrs.

McCormick, as we sat with our backs straight against our nailed-down, straight-in-a-row desks, with our arms stretched out in front of us, and with hands folded, that we we're going to change the world. There were more of us born in 1957 than ever before in the history of the world. We were told we were special and had to be smart.

Our being special and smart enough to memorize tons of facts and information may have served us well on standardized tests required for graduating from high school and entering college, but our *having to know* has made us some of the most unhappy and dissatisfied people in the history of the world. Statistically, my "Baby Boomer" generation has higher rates of chronic diseases, like diabetes and hypertension, and more physical and mental disabilities than members of our parents' generation. Is it possible that we are more stressed out than the generation that grew up during the Great Depression and World War II?

My mother would often say to me, "You may have book knowledge, but you don't have any common sense!" I'd get very angry at her for saying that, not understanding exactly what she meant, because how could a "know-it-all" not know something?! I thought she was calling me stupid. But, what she was really trying to do was to let me know that there are things in life that I would have to open up to learning about without the help of my memorized data, books, or intellect. She was trying to get me to understand the bigger truth about life -- which is, *it is not an intellectual exercise.*

## Embracing Vulnerability and Imperfection

The first time I truly experienced this wisdom of my mother was the first time I got my heart broken. I experienced it again when I had the first of three abdominal surgeries to remove invasive fibroid tumors. Then again, when I was dealing with my recall of having been sexually abused. From that painful episode, I'll never forget the wise words of a friend of mine, who I had called up after having been triggered by a passage in a self-help book for survivors. He said to me, "You can read all the books on all those shelves of yours, but you still are going to have to do what your therapist told you. Remember?" My response was, "Yes. I have to allow myself to sit in my pain, to feel it so I can eventually feel my joy." In other words, I had to stop reading about the healing process and just do it – without KNOWING!

Trying to know is totally about trying to be in control in order to avoid pain. Back to the schoolroom example, it's trying not to be embarrassed or labelled a dunce. But the truth is, you can't avoid pain on your healing journey, or be in charge of everything and everyone in order to heal. You would not make it challenging enough, or you would make it too challenging. As I've said before, God, the Universe, the Higher Self knows more than we do or can know. Unless we are willing to stop trying to control the healing and growth process by thinking we can know what's going to happen, we will continue to suffer. This is the common sense, or as I now call it "cosmic sense", that my mom was talking about all those years ago.

Letting go of having to know is not an easy task. It's also downright scary. It makes us vulnerable. Although we don't like feeling vulnerable, we can be grateful for Brené Brown, the research sociologist, whose TED Talk on the power of vulnerability went viral, landed her a guest spot on Oprah's show, and skyrocketed her career. Brené clearly spelled out from her research, that the people who were most resilient to life's challenges, were the ones who were able to be vulnerable. She's quoted as saying, "Vulnerability is the birthplace of innovation, creativity, and change." Her research evidenced that people who demonstrate a strong sense of love and belonging fully embrace vulnerability; they are courageous enough to be imperfect, authentic, and are comfortable with not knowing the ending of situations.

Stepping into a healing journey is no different than going on an adventure into the wilderness. You know there will be trees, mountains, lakes, and wild animals. You may even have a map of the landscape. But, you must still take the risk of not knowing what your experiences are truly going to be. Being alive means being vulnerable. Despite how much you may have been conditioned to always be certain, perfect, right, and in the know, you can unlearn this and embrace the truth. The truth being that you were born to be imperfect.

Our fear and disbelief in this truth will create great resistance to healing and growth, because that process is messy. The goal of healing is not to become perfect, but rather to become accepting and appreciative of the fact that you are not perfect. As Mr. Rogers always said to his audience of children at the end of each broadcast, "... *people can love you exactly the way you are.*" The challenge is to be willing to love yourself despite your limitations, imperfections, not having all the answers.

# Chapter 14

## Letting Go and Letting Come

### The Challenge of Change

C hange. The reason why we can heal from emotional pain and trauma is because of the natural, involuntary impulse for change. Yet, change is one of the biggest fears we face in life.

When I was about nine years old, I had a pair of Mary Jane-style red leather shoes. I loved those shoes. They made me happy, and I felt pretty when wearing them. Then one day, I put them on and my big toes were pushing so tightly up against the red leather that it hurt. But, I didn't care. These were my favorite shoes, and I loved them. I was not going to allow a little pain to keep us apart.

Well, each day that I continued to put them on, my feet would hurt a little more, then a little more. Finally, my mother noticed that I was walking awkwardly. She looked at me with that puzzled look I dreaded, then she looked back down at my shoes and asked, "Chile, what's wrong with your feet? Come here!" She investigated by feeling the tips of my shoes and could feel my toes pleading to burst out of their red leather prison. "Gurrll!" she half sighed, and half laughed. "These shoes are too small! Take them off! I've got to buy you some new shoes!" You can't imagine my great disappointment and upset over having to let go of those shoes that I loved so much. Those red leather shoes, for which I was willing to tolerate so much pain.

This story is a simple and deep illustration of how hard it is to accept growth and change. I can't tell you how many people have reached out to me to help them heal their emotional pain, yet cancel before starting the work, or stop when they feel the change from their healing is about to take hold of their lives. I accept and understand that one must be ready, willing, and able to let the fear go and let the change come. Just like I couldn't make those red shoes grow with my feet, there's no going back once change has taken hold of you and your life.

So, let's take a look at three of the primary reasons why stepping into a change and growth process is so challenging:

1. **You will be disrupted** – emotionally, intellectually, physically, and spiritually. Change means that you can't think, do, or be what you have been. When you try to go back to what you've known, you will experience painful consequences. This pain will be almost impossible to ignore.

2. **You will be messy.** Change not only disrupts, but it also creates mess. You will have to learn new ways of thinking, doing, and being. This means unlearning what you have learned that doesn't support the change. You'll have to discover what works for the new stuff that shows up, and you won't be able to easily practice or follow your usual routines. You may become scattered in your thoughts, feelings, and behaviors. Sometimes you'll choose the wrong situation and will have to start all over again. Sometimes you'll convince yourself that you can try to go back to what you knew, even though it will be painful. Despite your efforts to avoid the messiness of change, things will fall apart!

3. **You won't belong.** Change can create a disconnection between you and those who can't or won't support you in your process. No one likes to be put out of the tribe. Change brings an experience of loneliness that makes us feel unsafe and unloved.

# The Benefits of Change

Now, let's look at the three benefits of stepping into the change process. This is the treasure in the trouble:

1. *Disruptions is movement away from the pain body as your boss.* It is evidence that you are truly working on self-mastery. Disruption is the necessary battle between holding onto the pain and learning how to let it go.

2. *Messiness is evidence of something dying so something can be reborn.* Messiness means you are going through the process of transformation, transmutation and transcendence. It is breaking through to more of the truth of who you are. Messiness is letting go of the old ways that no longer serve you. The reward is your ability to discover the new ways that can support your experiences of your happy endings in life.

3. *When you no longer fit into the old group this means you've outgrown them.* Belonging to them will not support your growth and transformation. This means there is a new group of friends and supporters waiting for you. By letting go of the old you let come the new. At first you will grieve the old friends, but then you will celebrate the new ones. If it is family members from whom you become disconnected, know that as you accept the new, healed you completely, so will they. This is cosmic law.

One of my favorite fairytales from the Brothers Grimm collection is an excellent illustration of the letting go—letting come process. It is called, *Star-Money.*

> *There was once upon a time a little girl whose father and mother were dead, and she was so poor that she no longer had any little room to live in, or bed to sleep*

*in, and at last she had nothing else but the clothes she was wearing and a little bit of bread in her hand which some charitable soul had given her. She was, however, good and pious. And as she was thus forsaken by all the world, she went forth into the open country, trusting in the good God.*

*Then a poor man met her, who said: "Ah, give me something to eat, I am so hungry!" She reached him the whole of her piece of bread and said: "May God bless it to thy use," and went onwards. Then came a child who moaned and said: "My head is so cold, give me something to cover it with." So, she took off her hood and gave it to him; and when she had walked a little farther, she met another child who had no jacket and was frozen with cold. Then she gave it her own; and a little farther on one begged for a frock, and she gave away that also. At length she got into a forest and it had already become dark, and there came yet another child, and asked for a little shirt, and the good little girl thought to herself: "It is a dark night, and no one sees thee, thou canst very well give thy little shirt away," and took it off, and gave away that also.*

*And as she so stood, and had not one single thing left, suddenly some stars from heaven fell down, and they were nothing else but hard smooth pieces of money, and although she had just given her little shirt away, she had a new one which was of the very finest linen. Then she gathered together the money into this and was rich all the days of her life.*

This simple tale is a delicious teaching of how we must release and empty out in order to receive the new. The dead parents in the story may represent what can no longer serves us. The items of clothing may be representative of the thoughts, ideas, and beliefs that we have to shed in order for healing to occur. And finally, the *star-money* I see that as representing our healing treasure. It's our happy endings or fulfillment of our healing goals, dreams and wishes. It also represents our freedom from the burden of emotional pain.

On our journey to healing, it is so important that we stay conscious of the process. Remember "Thing One and Thing Two," the pain body and the trauma mind, are going to put up a good fight to maintain power and control over you. They will directly or covertly set up sabotaging situations for which you will need to be on the lookout. This is perhaps the most important reason why we need guides and helpers for our journey. We cannot make it through the change all alone. As Professor Dumbledore says many times to Harry Potter, *"Help will always come to those who deserve it!"* Just the fact that you are on a healing journey qualifies you for the help. So, let go and let come!

# Chapter 15

## The 5 Keys to Self-Mastery

### Unlocking Higher Consciousness

*J* n the second installment of the *Pirates of the Caribbean* films, "The Deadman's Chest", the audience is reintroduced to the character of *Jack Sparrow* as he is searching for a key. His crew has been impatiently waiting for him to return from a Turkish prison, and they are very angry that all he has to show them is a drawing of an elaborate key. He attempts to quell their anger and reassure them that he will lead them to treasure and asks them, "What do keys do?" The response from one of the crew members is, *"Keys unlock things?"* The crew member's response is in the form of a question, but for the purposes of Wisdom Walking, it needs to be a clear and truthful statement: KEYS UNLOCK THINGS!

As the film progresses, and even throughout the third film, the key that Jack Sparrow is seeking plays an enormously important role. Like all magical keys, it unlocks so much more than the chest of *Davey Jones*. I won't spoil anymore of the plot of this movie, in case you haven't seen it. However, if you have, you'll get a faster understanding of the point I'm making regarding the symbolic power of keys to unlock things. The final preparation piece for making the Wisdom Walk journey is to become familiar with the five keys to self-mastery:

1. **Meditation**, the key to the inner landscape or innerscape
2. **Contemplation**, the key to the domain of the pain body
3. **Affirmation**, the key to a big fat YES!

4. **Revelation**, the key to hidden truths
5. **Salvation**, the key to your personal freedom

These five keys are the tools, spiritual technology and experiences for moving forward along your wisdom walk. This healing journey will take you to the five elemental landscapes of the Dagara Medicine Wheel, which I will discuss in more detail in the coming chapters. In each of these elemental landscapes, the five keys will enable you to engage with and learn from the healing challenges found there. For example, in the landscape of Fire, the healing challenge is forgiveness of others and yourself. The five keys work together to support your ability to experience forgiveness and receive the gifts that this loving posture can bring into your life.

The essential power of the five keys to self-mastery is their ability to shift, grow, and raise your consciousness. As I discussed previously, the understanding of healing as moving forward to a higher consciousness is quite ancient. Philosophies and practices about enlightenment, also called *spiritual liberation*, can be found in every ancient wisdom and religious text around the world. A higher state of consciousness provides humans with the ability to transcend negativity and all forms of pain and suffering. It creates the absence of fear. It enables one to embrace the presence of Love.

Now, unlike the great spiritual teachers such as Buddha, Mohammed and Jesus Christ, most humans can only obtain and stay in higher consciousness for brief periods of time. But even if the "Nirvana" (the ancient Sanskrit word for spiritual liberation) lasts for only a nanosecond, its "love power" will have a lasting impact upon your mind, body and spiritual consciousness. It transforms you away from despair and into someone with unbounded hope. It enables you to choose love over fear and be a giver rather than just a taker. This is what I believe to be personal freedom.

Accessing a higher consciousness can be learned and

practiced with the help of the five keys. They work in synchronized order, like the steps in a dance. You begin with the practice of meditation which opens you up to the practice of contemplation. Through your contemplative practice, you will gain clarity about why you are suffering and what inside of you needs healing right now. With these insights, you are now in the position to wholeheartedly experience a spiritual affirmation by making a faith gesture through an elemental ritual. As a result of your affirmation that you are worthy of help from a greater order and direction than your own, you will automatically experience revelations. As these higher and deeper awarenesses are brought to light, you will automatically gain the ability to participate in situations where you can experience an end to your suffering.

Anyone willing to be free from emotional pain, and the suffering it creates, can successfully use the five keys. As a human being, you possess the inborn ability to grow, to heal, to recreate yourself — to evolve. When you remember this divine and cosmic truth, you are open to experience the truth of who you are. The following is a defining of each of the 5 keys and what your expectations can be in using each of them.

## Meditation: The Key to the Inner Landscape (Innerscape)

There is an invisible yet powerful world inside each of us. I call it the inner landscape or innerscape. As I shared in Chapter 4, this internal world remains locked in your unconscious. It requires a key to unlock it, and meditation is that key. I define meditation as shifting your attention away from your external situation and onto your internal situation. The goal of meditation is to quiet your worries, fears, anxieties, doubts and control dramas. Meditation accomplishes this by taking you into the present moment. Most people believe that meditation is hard to do, but that's not really true. Meditation is quite simple, and it makes you feel really good during and after you experience it. It's getting into a meditative state that is challenging.

The practice of meditation has been studied and results show that it helps to reduce stress, lower blood pressure, improve breathing, strengthen the immune system, and contribute greatly to overall feelings of wellness. So why is it so hard to get into? It's hard because it requires getting still and staying still while first listening to stress-filled thoughts before you can be at peace. Getting still in a world that demands things move faster and faster every day is quite a challenge. This is even more difficult when moving faster is associated with survival and winning. Getting still initially translates into being a loser, and in the extreme to dying. My expectation with meditation for wisdom walking is that you begin slowly and not judge yourself as you learn the art and practice of becoming present.

When I first learned to meditate, I could only keep still physically for five minutes. I made a commitment to myself to increase my stillness to one minute more each week. I used the stop watch on my cell phone. Slowly but surely, I was able to sit still without being agitated for 30 minutes. Next, I began to practice quieting my fear-talking mind. I discovered that as soon as I got still, fear-filled thoughts came flooding into my brain. I've always liked the 23rd Psalm from the Old Testament of the Bible (which I've edited below to be gender inclusive):

> *The Lord is my shepherd; I shall not want;*
> *He maketh me lie down in green pastures:*
> *He leadeth me beside the still waters.*
> *She restoreth my soul:*
> *She leadeth me on the paths of righteousness, for Her namesake.*

*Yea, though I walk through the Valley of the Shadow*
*of Death,*
*I shall fear no evil: for thou art with me;*
*Thy rod and thy staff they comfort me.*
*Thou preparest a table before me In the presence of*
*mine enemies:*
*Thou anointest my head with oil; my cup runneth over.*
*Surely, goodness and mercy shall follow me all the*
*days of my life:*
*And I shall dwell in the house of the Lord forever.*
*Amen, Ashe!*

I would silently recite that to myself over and over and over until the fear-talking stopped, and I could just relax and breathe.

I believe that the practice of meditation is a very natural thing for anyone to do. It doesn't matter if you use calming music, guided meditation apps, or the sound of drums and heartbeats. The main thing is that you bring yourself into the realm of your soul, and that you are calm, relaxed, and present. Once you have entered your inner landscape, you are now ready to do some contemplation of your emotional pain.

## Contemplation - The Key to the Pain Body Domain

The most common definition of contemplation is to examine, study and scrutinize something over a period of time. For the purpose of the Wisdom Walk, I define contemplation as asking the hard questions to and about your Self. Yes, I'm talking about the hard and painful questions that we really would rather not ask, and to which we definitely don't want to hear any answers. Of course, unless we are brave enough to ask and hear the truth, we will remain at the beck and call of our pain body, and the trauma-mind that empowers it.

In the second installment of *The Matrix Trilogy*, "The Matrix Reloaded", one of the most important characters is simply named, *The Key Maker*. He is the only entity that can give the story's hero, *Neo*, access to the control room of *The Architect* (Ruler) of the Matrix. Only by confronting the ruler of the Matrix can *Neo* fulfill his mission to stop the war between machines and humans. Now, let's imagine that this *Architect*, the supreme ruler of the illusionary world, is your pain body with the power to wage never-ending war over your life. Now, imagine *The Key Maker* and his keys as the power of contemplation to unlock the truth. As *Neo* discovers, using the key to open the *Architect's* strong hold does not stop the war, but it is an essential step towards cracking the code of the Matrix. In other words, the use of the Contemplation Key will give you access to the control room of your pain body and trauma-mind but ending your mental and emotional war will require three more keys. This includes enlisting the support of physical and non-physical guides and cheerleaders!

## Affirmation - The Key to a Big Fat 'YES'

Transforming pain, especially embedded pain from childhood adverse experiences and traumas, requires more than thinking and speaking about what happened to you. Both ancient wisdom and cutting-edge psychotherapy agree that trauma resolution is not just an intellectual exercise. Post-traumatic stress symptoms are rooted in the central nervous system, which means every cell of the body. So, when every cell in your body is saying 'No' to you having your happy endings in life, how do you get to a 'Yes'? Well, this is the purpose of the Affirmation Key.

If you've been practicing self-help before reading this book, you are probably familiar with the use of positive affirmations to focus your attention away from negative thoughts. Unlike this helpful intellectual tool, the Affirmation Key is a process that combines the power of your mind, your body, and your spiritual consciousness. By combining the power of your mind with a physical gesture of faith in yourself and the support of a spiritual container, the cells in your body can be cleansed of negativity in an energetic manner. The proof of this invisible transformation will become evident by the shift in your attitude from despair to hope. I call this process, making faith gestures, because it is a way to demonstrate with your whole self that you are worthy of having your pain transformed so you can live a life renewed and full of promise.

This way of getting to a big fat 'YES' about having your happy endings is rooted in the wisdom of the elemental rituals of the Dagara Medicine Wheel. I discuss this in greater detail in Part Four of this book. What's important to know right now is that you can learn to transform stuck pain just by being willing to do so. You do not have to believe in the Medicine Wheel, or a God, or even your soul in order to make an Affirmation. Spiritual medicine doesn't require your permission to do what it's divinely designed to do. Here's why:

*Just your willingness to learn how not to have your pain body running your life is enough to set in motion a series of events that will grant you healing. Right this moment you are breathing, and this is involuntary. You are not making it happen. The same is true for your heart beating and the thousands of other physical and non-physical functions that are all working together in this very moment to keep you alive. One of the most powerful of these functions is the ecstatic evolutionary impulse of the Universe. You are meant to be able to heal your pain, grow your emotional intelligence, and live a life full of joy, happiness, and love. Through the affirmation process, you can and will experience a BIG FAT 'YES'.*

## Revelation - The Key to Hidden Truths

Always, always, always after you have made a faith gesture through an elemental ritual, you will receive a revelation. Something insightful and enlightening about yourself and your situation will be revealed to you. These gifts of greater knowledge and clarity about your true self are unique. Sometimes they show up quietly in a dream, or through a conversation with someone you trust. Sometimes they hit you like a bolt of lightning. One man in the *Wisdom Walk to Self-Mastery* program had just such an experience. Shortly after participating at the last minute in a Fire Ritual where he made a faith gesture to be in charge of his pain body, he experienced a powerful transformation.

The ritual occurred on a Thursday afternoon, and our next class would not be held until the following Tuesday. When he arrived in class that Tuesday, the other men didn't recognize him. The usually non-verbal man, who looked like an imitation of 'Pig Pen' from the Charlie Brown comics, was gone. His clothes were cleaned up, dreadlocks cut off to reveal his entire face, and he couldn't wait to share with the healing community about his metamorphosis.

He described how it began the Friday night after the ritual when he was all alone in his apartment. Out of nowhere, he began to hear the sound of the djembe drumming as I had done for the ritual. The sound was so clear and real that he looked throughout his apartment, and even outside of his front door in his attempt to find the source. When no physical evidence for the drumming could be found, he accepted that it was a spiritual message. He said he realized that it was an important message.

So, he went through his apartment and gathered up all of his stashed and hidden drugs, paraphernalia, and alcohol, and threw them into the dumpster of his apartment building. He probably had thought many times about letting go of his drug and alcohol addiction, but this night he was able to take an important step toward making that happen. He was able to reconnect with his true self and defied his pain body. I saw this man about three years later, and he was still sober, still cleaned up, and living his truth.

## Salvation - The Key to Personal Freedom

When your pain body has been allowed to take charge of your life, it's not a good day. To survive, the pain body needs negative emotions to feed upon, so it will continuously attract negative people and situations into your life. This brings suffering into your experience. By using the first four keys to self-mastery wholeheartedly, and in their proper sequence, you can experience an end to a suffering. The power of getting still and meditating opens the door to the power of contemplating and confronting the pain, which leads to the ability to affirm your ability to transform the negative into a positive, which opens the door to the revelations connected to the truth of who you are, along with your belief in your worthiness to live happily and with love. This fifth key of Salvation is the higher consciousness that you can access as a result of your healing process.

The experience of the Salvation Key is the experience of personal freedom. Knowing that you can choose to put your pain body in its place frees you up from being a victim to life. The absence of suffering leaves our mind and emotions with the time and energy to create new experiences and engage in new and right situations and relationships. Through the achievement of salvation you will have more insight, wisdom and energy to support and grow your capacity for well-being, kindness, compassion, creativity, joy and love.

In the next five chapters, I will take you on the journey through the landscape of the Wisdom Walk. I will apply the five keys to self-mastery to each of the Dagara Medicine Wheel elemental landscapes. By continuing to read this next part of the book, you are agreeing to experience a mental, emotional, and spiritual shift. There's no going back, so make sure you have the proper gear -- an open mind, an open heart, and a willingness to transform your pain. Ashé!

# Part Four
# THE WISDOM WALK HEALING JOURNEY

# INTRODUCTION

*D*ear Reader, you have arrived at the portal of the *Wisdom Walk to Self-Mastery* healing journey. The book will escort you through the five elemental landscapes which are: the Ancestral Mountain of Fire, the Valley of Water, the Earth Village, the Mineral Portal, and the Land of Nature. Each elemental landscape provides the opportunity for you to address embedded emotional pains and the emotional barriers and blocks they create to having happy endings in life.

These blocks and barriers are universal and archetypal, meaning that they are experienced and understood by all human beings. Everyone at some point in their lifetime will have their heart broken, will feel invalidated by those they love, with feel shame, or will resist change with all their might. When you enter the realm of an elemental landscape, you will be presented with the opportunity to use the 5 Keys to Self-Mastery to heal your emotional pain.

At the entrance of each elemental landscape, you will be encouraged to meditate for 15 minutes. If you haven't meditated before or would like assistance, I've included a link to my website where you'll find meditation videos that I've created for your convenience. When you've completed your meditation, return to the book where you will find an overview of the healing challenge of the elemental landscape you are visiting. This will be followed by contemplative questions. Then, when you feel ready for an affirmation, the book will guide you to make a faith gesture through a personal ritual using the elemental wisdom of the Dagara Medicine Wheel. You will also receive post-ritual guidance. Once you've received insights and clarity from the experience of transforming your pain, you'll be encouraged to make note of them before moving on to the next landscape. I've also provided links to videos where I will acknowledge your progress and cheer you on through each elemental landscape.

The Wisdom Walk healing journey is sequential, meaning it is designed to follow the cosmic evolutionary order of the 5 elements. It begins with Fire and ends with Nature. This healing process is also developmental, with one healing challenge leading to another. I highly recommend that you follow this order for your journey. Of course, you may follow your own intuition for what may work best for you.

Most importantly, **TAKE YOUR TIME!**
**DO NOT RUSH THE PROCESS!**

This healing journey is full of transformation and manifestation. You have to want it right more than just wanting to get through it. For example, if you do your personal ritual and make your faith gesture but don't receive any insights or clarity for a week or two, that's okay. Your revelations and experience of salvation will show up. All of this, on your part, is a choice. So choose to get free from your pain. Finally, it's important that you make sure that you are fulfilled and complete before moving from one healing challenge on to the next. That's just plain good cosmic sense.

**My Prayer for Your Journey:**

*As you embark on your Wisdom Walk healing journey,*
*I call upon your Ancestors,*
*Spirit Guides,*
*Non-physical Teachers,*
*and Loving Entities that walk with you and guide your every step;*
*May your Greater Order and Direction,*
*your God,*
*bring you the courage, patience and faith you need*

*to transform that which can no longer serve you.*
*May you receive profound revelations*
*and know the sweetness of the salvation,*
*which is promised to all who say,*
*"I'm willing to receive:*
*Thank you, Thank you, Thank you!"*
*May this be true, always.*
*Ashé! Ahau! Amen!*

# Chapter 16

# The Ancestral Mountain of Fire

## Key #1 - MEDITATION:

*T*o support your willingness to transform your emotional pain, I ask at this point that you get still and meditate for at least 15 minutes. The meditative process helps you more easily access your inner landscape. I have recorded a meditation to specifically help you prepare for the inner work of this elemental landscape. Here's the link to my website: www.wisdomwalktoselfmastery.com

Click on "Book Videos" and select *Ancestral Mountain of Fire Meditation.*

## Overview of the Elemental Landscape

The Ancestral Mountain of Fire symbolizes the emotional wounds that are inherited from your family of origin. Most people do not realize that they have eight (8) great-grandparents. These are the people whose life experiences, beliefs, traditions and culture greatly influenced the family into which you were born. Even if you are not able to know exactly who these ancestors were, you can use history and the average age of childbearing to understand what their life may have been like.

Suppose that your parents were born in the 1960s. By subtracting 20 years for each preceding generation, you'll have a good idea as to when your great-grand parents were born. Parents born in the 1960s, means grandparents born in the 1940s, means great-grand parents born in the 1920s. So if your great-grand parents were born in the 1920s, they grew up dealing with the Great Depression and World War II. This was a time of struggling and suffering for everyone, but certain groups of people were severely challenged in their daily lives in regards food, shelter, work, and health. The ways in which your great-grand parents viewed the world and their position in it would have strongly influenced the culture of your family. Their having to be in survival mode would have left little or no time to express, or let alone, process painful emotions. These unexpressed emotions would have leaked out into the home and family in some very painful ways. Remember, *any pain that is not transformed will be transferred.*

In the Ancestral Mountain of Fire, you can choose to become more aware of and break through cycles of inherited pain. In this elemental landscape you become conscious of or validated in how your family wounds, and also cultural wounds, are contributing to your present-day pain body. Any form of abuse, sexual, physical, mental, or emotional, that was experienced by your ancestors and not processed and transformed, got passed down to the next generations --which does include you. Often, this pain is re-enacted by parents onto their children. This creates a perpetual cycle of dysfunction, abuse, addictions and chronic diseases in families and communities.

## The Healing Challenge: FORGIVENESS

Forgiveness is the most powerful grace you can receive for healing ancestral wounds. It is not an intellectual exercise. It is not about letting anyone off the hook for the wrong they have done. Forgiveness is all about releasing the pain that was transferred onto you. It's also the opportunity to transform the pain you have transferred onto others.

Forgiveness is a challenge because you don't really know how to forgive anyone, and they don't really know how to forgive you. I don't believe our human minds have that ability. When someone hurts you very deeply, or you hurt someone very deeply, it's really hard to even imagine saying "I forgive you" or asking for forgiveness. You need non-intellectual and non-physical help to experience authentic forgiveness.

Forgiveness is truly a divine act that is freeing in a way most people can't even imagine, until it is experienced. You cannot think your way to forgiveness. Your heart and soul must be involved and present. So, for this reason, forgiveness is a grace you must ask for from a Greater Order and Direction and then open yourself up to receive. Forgiveness, as a divine energy, once received, infuses every cell of your body, every quantum wave of your emotional psyche, with pure unconditional love. To receive the grace of forgiveness, you need only to be willing. Especially when you think you can never forgive someone or forgive yourself, just be willing to have it happen. Just be willing to wake up one morning and have the attachment to the pain and suffering be gone. Your God and the Universe will handle the details.

Now, it's important to know and remember that the practice of forgiving others and yourself is not a one-time event. It is a process that you repeat over and over again until your attachment to the pain of the past is no longer present. When you become willing to receive the grace of forgiveness, and have the experience of the pain being gone, if you think about or come into contact with the person you forgave or who forgave you, but there is still a feeling of judgement, resentment or blame, more forgiveness work is required. You'll know when you are complete with your forgiveness practice because there will no longer be any form of attachment to what others did to you, or what you did to others.

# Emotional Barriers and Blocks to Be Overcome

1. Ignoring the "skeletons in the family closet"
2. Carrying other people's pain
3. Staying stuck in old beliefs

<u>Ignoring the Skeletons in the Family Closet</u>

Hidden family wounds, or "skeletons in the closet," have a way of manifesting themselves through the behaviors of the persons considered the "black sheep" of the family. These are the persons who become alcoholic and/or drug addicted, who perpetrate abuse and violence, who find it hard to get and keep a regular job, who lie, cheat, and steal. I call these family members the *Wound Walkers.* You hate to see these people coming. You have such anger at them and you're ashamed to be related to them. The truth is though, that something in you knows, *there, but for the Grace of God, go I!* Which means, you could be the "black sheep" of the family because you have the same DNA. According the wisdom of the Dagara culture, these family members are bearing and bringing a message of the unhealed pain within the family. Once they can be recognized as cosmic messengers, instead of mistakes, the healing process can begin. What they are manifesting outwardly is residing within you silently and unconsciously. It's called your pain body.

There are countless stories of people who become materially and financially successful only to fall into drug addiction, sexual perversion, criminal activity, or other scandalous behavior. They fail at their ability to be emotionally healthy and morally fit. Money, even fame, cannot heal ancestral wounds, or keep them from busting out all over. In fact, financial and material success can make the wounds grow into fire-breathing monsters! Ignoring the painful, shameful things from the family's past will not make them go away.

## Carrying Other People's Pain

Another way to think of this barrier to your emotional well-being is about being co-dependent by taking on someone else's pain. When you take on someone else's pain, probably believing that this will help them, you distract yourself from dealing with your own pain. Transferred pain can never do anyone any good. This co-dependency can also show up between you and your ancestors. Dr. Mary Yellow Horse Brave Heart, an expert on the impact of historical trauma upon Native Americans, is the first person I ever heard talk about being loyal to the suffering of the ancestors. In other words, having your happy endings in life seems like a betrayal because of all the horror and suffering that your ancestors went through. This is associated with survivor guilt, which is a form of historical post-traumatic stress syndrome, or the pain body being allowed to run the show for the family, as well as their community.

Truthfully, the last thing the ancestors want or need from you is a repeat of what they've already gone through. Holding onto the suffering of the ancestors is also a way to distract yourself from addressing your own pain. You can't tend to the fulfillment of your hopes and dreams by dragging around the pain of the past.

## Staying Stuck in Old Beliefs

Change is inevitable, but growth is optional. Everything changes, including beliefs and ways of understanding and doing things. Transcending the dysfunctional behavior associated with your ancestral wounds, and seriously breaking up cycles of abuse and violence, requires healing and growing into new ideas, new beliefs, and new ways of understanding and living your life. I've always loved this quote: *"If you always do what you've always done, you will always get what you've always gotten!"*

## Key #2 - CONTEMPLATION:

Please review and answer the following contemplative questions regarding the emotional barriers and blocks of the Ancestral Mountain of Fire. This is not a quiz. There are no right or wrong answers. This is for you to discover what you need to discover about your emotional barriers and blocks.

1. What do you believe happened to create the family wound?
2. What do you believe is the biggest wound within your family?
3. Who in your family is a Wound Walker?

   (If you spent time in foster care, or were adopted, and don't know enough about your family of origin, use the family or families who impacted you the most.)

4. How did family members transfer their pain onto you?
5. When you think of these experiences do you feel mad, sad, scared, or numb?
6. In what ways do you believe these painful experiences are blocking you from your happy endings in life?
7. Identify at least 3 things that you were taught about life that you think may be keeping you stuck in the past.
8. Identify at least 3 things that you were taught about yourself that may be creating emotional barriers to your happy endings in life.

# Key #3 - AFFIRMATION:

## Asking for Forgiveness with Fire Ritual

*The heat of the fire ritual also reminds us that heat is the circulation of energy. Life is manifested only when energy can circulate. The Dagara language uses the same word "di" (pronounced "dee") to mean "burn," "consume," and "eat." The connection is not, however, about destruction, but about transformation. Any person who goes through a fire ritual involves himself with transformation and change.*
— from The Healing Wisdom of Africa, by Malidoma Patrice Some, p.213

## Step 1: Prepare a symbol of what needs to be released

The element of Fire is a very radical energy for transforming pain. Whatever is placed into a fire will never look the same or be the same again. This occurs very quickly, within just a few minutes. Because of its radical nature, Fire is a powerful ally for breaking through resentment, judgement, and blame that can keep us attached to deep hurts.

Having done your contemplation of the three barriers and blocks to emotional wellness associated with the Mountain of Ancestral Fire, it's time to identify what within you is ready to be released and transformed by Fire. You'll begin by first calling on your ancestors. Ancestors can be called upon for all elemental rituals, but for Fire rituals it is essential.

Fire is believed to be the portal between this world and what the Dagara call "The Land of the Ancestors." In that realm, the souls are no longer bound to their Earthly reality. They get to review their sacred contracts to learn if they kept all of their promises, and to integrate the lessons from their lifetime. Having had the experience of being in the physical realm, they become available as non-physical wisdom guides and cheerleaders for those of us still Earth-bound. Their only hope is for us to not repeat their past wrongs, to win at being on purpose, and having our happy endings in life.

On one piece of paper, write down the names of all the ancestors you would like to support you with your faith gesture. Ancestors do not have to be blood related. They need only be persons who are no longer walking in a physical reality. They could have been friends of you and your family, or celebrities who have died and with whom you feel a strong connection. They could also be Wound Walkers, because they have a full understanding and appreciation for their sacred contracts. Now all they want to do is help you accomplish yours. Having walked on the dark side of the Force, they can be very helpful guides for what you need to avoid.

Once you've identified your Ancestor allies you are now ready to make your Forgiveness Lists. On another sheet of paper, you'll need to create two columns.

One column will be for listing all of the people you need to forgive. The other column will be for all the people you want to forgive you. You may use as much paper as needed for your two lists.

When that is completed, take one more piece of paper, and write out this affirmation request for your faith gesture:

> *Creator, All the One (however you address your God), enable me to receive your Grace of Forgiveness for my Self. Thank you, thank you, thank you.*

Finally, gather all of the papers you have written on, and roll them up. The Dagara believe that Spirit and the Ancestors love beauty, so you may place a nice ribbon or twine around your rolled paper. You can also wrap it in colored tissue paper or beautiful wrapping paper and garnish it with flowers. Place what is now your offering and reciprocity in a safe place, like an altar, where it won't be disturbed. You want to demonstrate that this bundle is sacred and worthy of respect.

## Step 2: Choosing and preparing right environment

Ideally, elemental rituals are performed outside in Nature. Personal rituals, especially for those living in urban areas, can be performed making the most out of that which you have to work. One of the first Fire rituals I facilitated for the men in the *Wisdom Walk to Self-Mastery* program was done using a moveable patio fire pit, in the parking lot behind the Alma Center, in the early afternoon. What's most important about the environment you use is that you intend for it to become a sacred space.

To make any space sacred, whether inside or outside of your home, you need to feel that you are safe from any harm, that you won't be interrupted, and that you have enough privacy. A sacred space is a respected place that supports your willingness to go in and connect with your heart and soul. Everything you do in a sacred space is to be done with a sense of confidence, respect, patience and love. There is no need to rush through the process.

Preparing a sacred space requires both physical and energetic arrangements. I suggest that you set up an Ancestor Altar. An altar is a visual reminder that you are in a sacred space engaging with a Greater Order and Direction. A very simple way to set up an Ancestor Altar is to lay out a red cloth on a table, counter or bureau, and place a safely burning red candle on it. Also, place on your altar any pictures of your ancestors and/or items that belonged to them. If you don't have any ancestor pictures or items in your possession, you can write the names of your ancestors on a piece of paper and place that on the altar instead. Last but not least, place your bundle to burn on the altar as well.

Once you've made your space sacred, you can decide how

you want to burn your bundle. Unless you have a fireplace, I do not recommend burning your bundle inside your home. It's best to go outside and use an actual fire pit, a grill, or a fire proof moveable fire pit. Preparing the place where you will do your fire ritual must also be done in a sacred manner with confidence, respect, patience, and love.

On a final note, the element of Fire can easily get out of control. It doesn't like to be confined or controlled as it does its transformation and transmutation work. Just as a precaution, whenever you work with fire in a sacred manner, it's best to not take any chances so have enough water or a fire extinguisher nearby.

## Step 3: The Invocation

An invocation is a prayer and an invitation to your God, your Ancestors, Guardian Angels, Spirit Guides, and Loving Entities to support you as you make your faith gesture through an elemental ritual. In calling forth the presence of the metaphysical, you are humbling yourself. You are admitting that you don't know how to transform your pain and that you need help. An invocation is also an expression of faith and gratitude for the help you need to receive. An invocation is most importantly said out loud. It is your vocal demonstration of your willingness to receive a healing grace.

Here is an example of a simple invocation that I have used to initiate making a faith gesture using the element of Fire:

> *Creator, Mother-Father-God, Source, All-the-One, All That Is, I'm calling out to you to come and be with me right now, as I open myself to your greater Will. I thank you for my Ancestors, Spirit Guides, and Loving Entities, and knowing I cannot do this alone, I also call on them to assist me in pushing my ego aside, remaining humble, and allowing your healing energy to take hold*

*of me. Thank you, thank you, thank you for what I am*
*about to receive, in the name of all that is Holy, I say*
*Amen, Ashé, Ahau, Asa, Ashinga, Bismillah!*

There is no right or wrong way to do an invocation. Just speak aloud from your heart, and let your soul do what it knows best – to be loving.

### Step 4: Making the Faith Gesture

Once you've said your invocation, you are now ready to burn your bundle and release what its contents symbolize. Everyone's experience of making their faith gesture is unique. I've never, in my almost 20 years of facilitating ritual, seen anyone do it the same way as anyone else. Your experience of burning your bundle, as a demonstration of your belief that your pain can be transformed into loving and generative energy, cannot be dictated by me or anyone else. The Dagara believe that Fire is a portal between this world and the Land of the Ancestors, and that when you offer your bundle to them, you are actually "feeding" them food that they need to be able to help you. This is why the bundle is considered reciprocity. You may want to think about that as you are making your faith gesture.

### Step 5: Gratitude and Closing

The final step in any elemental ritual is to take time to express gratitude. I always thank the element that has been my ally, as well as my ancestors, all my spirit guides, and of course my God. I also take a moment to check for how I'm feeling emotionally. I usually feel glad, good, relieved, and free. To close out the ritual, I clean up whatever needs cleaning and extinguish any candles with loving gratitude.

**Note:** *At the very end of this chapter, you will find a link to a video where I will acknowledge you for your work in the Ancestral Mountain of Fire and encourage you to continue on your Wisdom Walk healing journey.*

## Rewiring and Post-Ritual Care

The ancient technology of elemental ritual will have an effect on your mind, body and spirit. This healing process actually rewires your brain so that you can have access to new, positive, generative thoughts and ideas. As old patterns of thought are being disrupted and revised, you may experience some or all of the following physical symptoms:

- very tired and needing to lay down and take naps
- wired, and not easily going to sleep or staying asleep
- very hungry all the time
- no appetite at all
- flu-like symptoms, including fever
- irrational sadness or laughing.

This list is not complete. They may be other unusual things that you experience.

Just remember that these are all "natural" results of the deep and important work you did on yourself. Rewiring usually last about 3-5 days, but it can last a little longer. Everyone is unique in how they experience their post-ritual process.

During your rewiring process, do be gentle and nurturing with yourself. Slow things down and allow yourself to get as much rest and relaxation as you can. Getting a massage, reiki, acupuncture, or other supports for your physical health, will be really good to do. Also, do drink lots of water to flush out the toxins that you are now able to shed out of your system. Once the symptoms pass, you will feel very well and open to learning and doing even more to support the transformation of your pain.

# Key #4 - REVELATION:

## Staying Awake to Insights & Clarity

Once you've progressed through your rewiring process, you will get validation that your faith gesture has made a difference in your life. It is usual to have awareness of a shift in how you are feeling, thinking, believing, and what you are doing. As I stated in the previous chapter regarding the Revelation Key, the gifts of greater knowledge and clarity about your true self will be unique. Sometimes they show up quietly in a dream, or through a conversation with someone you trust. Sometimes they hit you like a bolt of lightning.

I suggest that you make note on a daily basis of what you are feeling, thinking, believing, and doing. By writing or recording what you are aware of, you will be growing your ability to be conscious of how the grace of *Forgiveness* is removing barriers and blocks to your happy endings in life.

# Key #5 - SALVATION:

## The End of the Suffering

The Universe truly is always working on your behalf. You will know that the Grace of Forgiveness has been given to you when you are no longer feeling attached to the pain you worked to transform. As I said before, the absence of suffering leaves your mind and emotions with the time and energy to create new experiences, new situations and better relationships. All of that supports and grows your capacity for well-being, kindness, compassion, creativity, joy and love.

# CONGRATULATIONS!

You have used all 5 of your keys to self-mastery and made it over the Ancestral Mountain of Fire. It's now time to travel down into the Valley of Waters and face the challenge of *Peacemaking*.

For a virtual acknowledgment of your progress, and encouragement for continuing your Wisdom Walk healing journey, click on the link below that will take you to my *Wisdom Walk to Self-Mastery* website. Once there, click on "Book Videos" to access the *Fire Ritual Praise*.

www.wisdomwalktoself-mastery.com

# Chapter 17

# The Valley of Still Waters

## Key #1 - MEDITATION:

*T*o support your willingness to transform your emotional pain, I ask at this point that you get still and meditate for at least 15 minutes. The meditative process helps you more easily access your inner landscape. I have recorded a meditation to specifically help you prepare for the inner work of this elemental landscape. Here's the link to my website www.wisdomwalktoself-mastery.com Once there, click on "Book Videos" to access *Valley of Still Waters Meditation.*

## Overview of the Elemental Landscape

The Valley of Still Waters symbolizes all of the feelings you've shut down in response to either physical and/or emotional pain. In this internal landscape we find the stagnant waters of uncried tears and unexpressed emotions. Here beside the still waters you meet up with the deep pain associated with loss.

Whether it is from a broken-heart, a betrayal, abandonment or domestic violence, your stuck pain can all be found here. The loss of a job, a home, a loved one, a limb, or your health are not experiences you recover from overnight, or all at once. That is why this internal valley contains the swamps of stuck grief, anger and rage. When left to fester and not transformed, this deep pain will shut us down to our feelings of joy and happiness. This loss of emotional intelligence creates anxiety, depression, and all forms of dysregulated (out-of-control) emotions and behaviors.

Entering the Valley of Still Waters is something we all dread doing. It's important to remember though, that you are not going to this valley to be a victim to your emotions and pain. You are going there to transform them and make peace with your past. You are wisdom walking through this landscape to reclaim your joy and happiness. There is a beautiful waterfall at the border leading out of this valley. This is the promise of the peacemaking and reconciliation you will experience by just being willing to release that which is blocking your happy endings from coming true.

## The Healing Challenge: PEACEMAKING

In the Valley of Still Waters, you will have the opportunity to free yourself from stuck negative emotions caused by loss. You will be guided to release your negative emotions in a peaceful way. As a result, you will experience inner peace.

There is shame, blame, and guilt associated with loss that puts us at odds with ourselves. We will question ourselves, become doubtful and suspicious about our existence. This inner conflict is sometimes referred to as, "the dark night of the soul." The only way to win the battle is to make peace with the negative situation by accepting it, then learning how to feel and move through it in a loving and peaceful manner.

There is a force inside of you that knows how to do that. I call this force self-compassion. It can become your champion for overcoming your negativity, your pain body, that wields an energetic ability to cut you off from your experiences of joy and happiness. Self-compassion is when you've experienced a loss and choose to consciously grieve and make it through your pain using the power of Love. Self-compassion enables you step out of denial about your loss, to let go of believing that you're not supposed to suffer loss. In this peaceful manner, you open yourself up to finding the treasure in the unwanted change. When you choose to not blame and shame anyone for your loss, when you admit to any wrong-doing on your part that may have contributed to your loss, you are also being compassionate with yourself. This is also the experience of loving yourself unconditionally.

Your pain body and the negative emotions that it generates cannot exist in a loving environment. We often forget that a loving environment is our natural state. This means that the releasing of your fear-based thoughts and beliefs will result in you accessing self-love and inner peace. Like forgiveness, peacemaking isn't a one-time event. This means you will not have to feel and release all of your stuck pain all at once. Having to deal with your pain is never a picnic, but remember, choosing to feel and release it enables you to make peace with your past, so it doesn't become your future.

# Emotional Barriers and Blocks to Be Overcome

1. Shame
2. Blame
3. Guilt

Shame

The experience of loss creates a disruption to what makes us feel secure in who we are in relation to others and the world. The loss of a job, a home or relationship is always accompanied by shame. Shame is the proverbial *wet blanket* to living a life of joy and happiness. You experience shame not just from having done something wrong, but also from having something wrong done to you.

Shame prohibits you from being your authentic self. It

constantly tells you, "There's something wrong with you." This negative belief will compel you to prove that you are not. The goal of proving what you are not attracts more of what you are not. Unwise choices are usually involved in how you deal with shame. For example, a common solution many shame-filled people take to avoid their pain is to join a religious organization. Joining anything out of fear will not have good consequences.

A shame-filled person makes a one-way bargain to follow the dictates of something outside of themselves, such as a person, a community or an institution, to relieve their pain. They take on people-pleasing in a big way and find it hard to set boundaries. Unfortunately, this is a distraction. The shame will get covered over by the external focus on doing what's believed to be required to belong to the person, community, or institution. The focus will not be on transforming the shame, but on doing what seems to be required to be considered a good person. This isn't to say that joining a church can't support a healing process. It's just that shame can't be resolved by memorizing holy texts and not giving oneself permission to say "NO"!

When you put your attention on proving who you are not, it leaves little or no attention on who you are really. "Happy Endings" in life, the ones that last, can only come from being your authentic self. Your authentic self emerges when you uncover your shame and consciously choose to release it.

Blame

Blaming someone for your loss will never make your loss come back. It seems that especially when the loss is unexpected, we go looking for blame. We put our focus on the external rather than going to our internal landscape to contemplate what might be the message from the loss. It is important to hold ourselves and others accountable for wrongdoings that result in the loss, especially loss of life. But, blaming is not the same as accountability. Blaming is seeing the person, or yourself, as being the negative behavior.

This same result occurs when you stay stuck in self-blame. When you were a child, and bad things happened around you and to you, blaming yourself was the only response your developing mind could offer. Like shame, blame tells you that you are bad. It works hard to convince you that you are something wrong that can never be right. As a result of believing these untruths, you will attract people and situations that support your blame game. Your blame game is also called self-hatred. There are no happy endings coming out of that!

Guilt

Feeling guilty about loss is another barrier to internal peacemaking. Like shame and blame, guilt also interferes with your ability to like, love and value yourself. Guilt, though, goes one step further in the development of self-hatred. It tells you that you are not worthy or deserving of fulfillment in life.

Guilt, even more than shame or blame, really fuels self-sabotage. It loves to lie and wait until you have achieved a level of success and happiness. Then, BAM!! It brings out the wrecking ball to disrupt and demolish all of your best efforts.

Guilt can be cyclical, meaning it can go into life-long repetition. The cycle of guilt is sustained when you silently blame yourself and invite shame to come along for the ride. Silently blaming and shaming yourself means you are not taking any conscious steps to lovingly address your loss. Guilt that is embraced, held onto, will keep you imprisoned in the past. We hold onto guilt not only because we may not know how to transform it, but also because we don't think we deserve to have it transformed. You will not be able to believe that you can reinvent your life and create as many happy endings as you need, if guilt is your constant companion.

# Key #2 - CONTEMPLATION:

Please review and answer the following contemplative questions regarding the emotional barriers and blocks of the Valley of Still Waters. This is not a quiz. There are no right or wrong answers. This is for you to discover what you need to discover about your emotional barriers and blocks.

1. What is something you loss that still brings you feelings of shame?
2. Who is someone you loss that still brings you feelings of shame?
3. What is something that happened to you for which you are most ashamed?
4. What is something that you've done for which you are most ashamed?
5. Who do you blame the most for your unhappiness in life, and why?
6. Is anyone blaming you for their unhappiness, and if so, why?
7. What's something in life for which you blame yourself, and continue to feel guilty about?
8. How is your unresolved shame, blame and guilt blocking your success, happiness, peace, or fulfillment in life? What might it be keeping you from doing, having, and being in life?

# Key #3 - AFFIRMATION:

## Asking for Peacemaking with Water Ritual

*Water rituals tie up loose ends. These loose ends are obstacles to our balance and reconciliation, our peace and serenity...*

— from The Healing Wisdom of Africa, by
Malidoma Patrice Some, p.218

## Step 1: Prepare a symbol of what needs to be released

The element of Water can provide a gentle transformation of the pain we are holding from loss. Water has the ability to dissolve things over a period of time. The slow cleansing of stuck pain makes our grief experience more bearable.

Having done your contemplation of the three barriers and blocks to emotional wellness in the landscape of the Valley of Still Waters, it's time to identify what within you is ready to be released and transformed by the Water element. You'll begin by first calling on the Ancestors. Ancestors can be called upon for all elemental rituals. For water rituals, calling on your female ancestors is very appropriate.

Calling on the Ancestors for support is ancient tradition practiced by all indigenous cultures. The Dagara believe that the deceased leave this realm and return to the parallel world they call "The Land of the Ancestors." In that realm, the souls are no longer bound to their Earthly reality. They get to review their sacred contracts to learn if they kept all of their promises, and to integrate the lessons from their lifetime. Having had the experience of being in the physical realm, they become available as wisdom guides for those of us still Earth-bound. Their only hope is for us to not repeat their past wrongs, to win at being on purpose, and having our happy endings in life.

Once you have connected with your female ancestors, you will be ready to write out lists, draw some pictures, or fabricate some organic symbols of what you are ready to heal regarding shame, blame, and guilt. However you decide to create the symbols of your healing, know that you will be putting them into a bundle. The Dagara believe that Spirit loves beauty, and female Water spirits definitely appreciate receiving bundles that are pleasing to the eye. So, make your bundles out of lovely-looking wrapping paper or cloth. You may also garnish it with flowers. When in doubt about what paper or cloth to use, know that both blue and black are appropriate, as these are the colors associated with the Water element in the Dagara Medicine Wheel.

Before you tie up your bundle, write out and include this affirmation request for your faith gesture:

> *Creator, All the One (however you address your God),*
> *enable me to receive your Grace of Peacemaking within*
> *my Self. Thank you, thank you, thank you.*

Place what is now your offering or reciprocity in a safe place, like an altar, where it won't be disturbed. You want to demonstrate that this bundle is sacred and worthy of respect.

## Step 2: Choosing and preparing right environment

Ideally, elemental rituals are performed outside in Nature. Personal water rituals, even for those living in urban areas, should be done by a lake, a river, a sea, or the ocean. The bigger the body of water, the better. African cultures honor and associate water with the spirit of the Divine Feminine, such as Mami Wada from West Africa or Yemanjá in Brazil. When you invoke the Water element as a healing ally, you are taking your grief to the gentle and nurturing arms of a loving mother.

Making a faith gesture by a body of water may not always afford you complete privacy. But, you can still create a safe and sacred space to do your healing work through focus and intention. Of course you should find a spot that is off the beaten track. You may also want to go to the water at sunrise, or at a time when not many people will be around. I have done many personal rituals at the lakefront in Milwaukee without any problem. I've even had some people ask if they could participate. When you are focused and clear about your intention, people who notice you will respect your sacred space. A sacred space is a respected place that supports your willingness to go in and connect with your heart and soul. Everything you do in a sacred space is to be done with a sense of confidence, respect, patience and love. There is no need to rush through the process.

To energetically support your faith gesture at the water, I suggest that you first set up a Water Altar in your home. An altar is a visual reminder that you are in a sacred space engaging with a Greater Order and Direction. A very simple way to set up a Water altar is to lay out a blue cloth on a table, counter or bureau, and place a safely burning blue candle on it. Next, put some water in a small bowel or vessel and place that on your altar. Holding the water bowel or vessel and saying a prayer of gratitude to the water is also very helpful. You may also place sea shells, pictures of water, and any other symbols of water. Last but not least, place your bundle on the altar until you are ready for your ritual.

### Step 3: The Invocation

An invocation is a prayer and an invitation to your God, your Ancestors, Guardian Angels, Spirit Guides, and Loving Entities, to support you as you make your faith gesture through an elemental ritual. In calling forth the presence of the metaphysical, you are humbling yourself. You are admitting that you don't know how to transform your pain and that you need help. An invocation is also an expression of faith and gratitude for the help you need to receive. An invocation is most importantly said out loud as your vocal demonstration of your willingness to receive a healing grace. Here is an example of a simple invocation I have used before making a faith gesture using the element of Water:

*Creator, Mother-Father-God, Source, All-the-One,*
*All That Is, I'm calling out to you to come and be*
*with me right now, as I open myself to your greater*
*Will. I thank you for my Ancestors, Spirit Guides, and*
*Loving Entities, and knowing I cannot do this alone,*
*I also call on them to assist me in pushing my ego*
*aside, remaining humble, and allowing your healing*
*energy to take hold of me. I also call upon the Spirit of*
*Water, in all her many forms, and ask that she receive*
*my bundle of pain to be transformed into inner peace.*
*Thank you, thank you, thank you for what I am about*
*to receive, in the name of all that is Holy, I say Amen,*
*Ashé, Ahau, Asa, Ashinga, Bismillah!*

There is no right or wrong way to do an invocation. Just speak aloud from your heart, and let your soul do what it knows best – to be loving.

## Step 4: Making the Faith Gesture

Once you've said your invocation, you are now ready to release your pain from loss, that is symbolized by your bundle into the body of Water. Everyone's experience of making their faith gesture is unique. I've never, in my almost 20 years of facilitating ritual, seen anyone do it the same way as anyone else. So, your experience of releasing your bundle into the water, as a demonstration of your belief that your pain can be transformed into loving and peaceful energy, cannot be dictated by me or anyone else. The Dagara believe that making this kind of an offering to the Water element enlivens it. You are allowing her to be of service to humanity in a very deep way. You may want to think about that as you are making your faith gesture.

## Step 5: Gratitude and Closing

The final step in any elemental ritual is to take time to express gratitude. I always thank the element that has been my ally, as well as my Ancestors, all of my Spirit Guides, and of course my God. I also take a moment to check for how I'm feeling emotionally. I usually feel glad, good, relieved, and free. To close out the ritual, you can take a drink of high vibrational water, like spring water.

Can you see the waterfall as you are leaving the Valley of Still Waters?

**Note:** *At the very end of this chapter, you will find a link and code to a video on my website where I will acknowledge you for your work in the Valley of Still Waters and encourage you to continue on your Wisdom Walk healing journey.*

## Rewiring and Post-Ritual Care

The ancient technology of elemental ritual will have an effect on your mind, body and spirit. This healing process actually rewires your brain so that you can have access to new, positive, and generative thoughts and ideas. As old patterns of thoughts are being disrupted and revised, you may experience some or all of the following physical symptoms:

- very tired and needing to lay down and take naps
- wired, and not easily going to sleep or staying asleep
- very hungry all the time
- no appetite at all
- flu-like symptoms, including fever
- irrational sadness or laughing.

This list is not complete. They may be other unusual things that you experience.

Just remember that these are all "natural" results of the deep and important work you did on yourself. Rewiring usually last about 3-5 days, but it can last a little longer. Everyone is unique in how they experience their post-ritual process.

During your rewiring process, do be gentle and nurturing with yourself. Slow things down and allow yourself to get as much rest and relaxation as you can. Getting a massage, reiki, acupuncture, or other supports for your physical health, will be really good to do. Also, do drink lots of water to flush out the toxins that you are now able to shed out of your system. Once the symptoms pass, you will feel very well and open to learning and doing even more to support the transformation of your pain.

## Key #4 - REVELATION:

### Staying Awake to Insights & Clarity

Once you've progressed through your rewiring process, you will get validation that your faith gesture has made a difference in your life. It is usual to have awareness of a shift in how you are feeling, thinking, believing, and what you are doing. As I stated in the previous chapter regarding the Revelation Key, the gifts of greater knowledge and clarity about your true self will be unique. Sometimes they show up quietly in a dream, or through a conversation with someone you trust. Sometimes they hit you like a bolt of lightning. I suggest that you make notes on a daily basis of what you are feeling, thinking, believing, and doing. By writing or recording what you are aware of, you will be growing your ability to be conscious of how *Peacemaking* is removing barriers and blocks to your happy endings in life.

# Key #5 - SALVATION:

## The End of the Suffering

The Universe truly is always working on your behalf. You will know that the Grace of Peacemaking has been given to you when you are no longer feeling attached to the pain you worked to transform. As I said before, the absence of suffering leaves your mind and emotions with the time and energy to create new experiences, new situations and better relationships. All of that supports and grows your capacity for well-being, kindness, compassion, creativity, joy and love.

# CONGRATULATIONS!

You have used all 5 of your keys to self-mastery and now the still waters in this valley can continue their flow to the cosmic ocean! It's now time to travel over to the Earth Village and face the challenge of *Valuing Yourself and Others*.

For a virtual acknowledgment of your progress, and encouragement for continuing your Wisdom Walk healing journey, click on the link below that will take you to my *Wisdom Walk to Self-Mastery* website. Once there, click on "Book Videos" to access the *Water Ritual Praise*.

www.wisdomwalktoselfmastery.com

# Chapter 18

# The Earth Village

## Key #1 - MEDITATION:

*T*o support your willingness to transform your emotional pain, I ask at this point that you get still and meditate for at least 15 minutes. The meditative process helps you more easily access your inner landscape. I have recorded a meditation to specifically help you prepare for the inner work of this elemental landscape. Here's the link to my website www.wisdomwalktoselfmastery.com

Once there, click on "Book Videos" and select *Earth Village Meditation.*

## Overview of the Elemental Landscape

The Earth Village symbolizes your internal capacity for healthy interpersonal relationships. This capacity is rooted within your essential nature as a human being. Every human has the need for a loving home, within a loving community, in which it feels wonderful to belong. Everyone human has the need for safety, security, nourishment, acknowledgment, validation, abundance and unconditional loving support. When these essential basic needs are taken care of, as you grow from a child to an adult, you will have a strong foundation for believing that you matter, that you are enough, and that you are not disposable.

From your journey through the Ancestral Mountain of Fire and the Valley of Still Waters, you know that unhealed ancestral wounds and the inability to release the grief from loss will wreck a home, a community, and a person. Having our essential basic needs met is a serious challenge for the majority of people in the modern world. When any of these needs have not been fulfilled in a healthy and positive manner, your capacity for valuing yourself and experiencing *right relations* (an indigenous phrase meaning *relationships that are beneficial*), will be limited. Your belief system will promote mistrust of yourself and others. You will believe that co-dependency is love because you will be in doubt of yourself as valuable. In many instances, a person with a shattered internal *Earth Village* can become convinced that happy endings only exist in fairytales.

## The Healing Challenge: VALUING YOURSELF and OTHERS

Valuing yourself means that you have the willingness and ability to have your essential basic needs fulfilled. It means you have a loving relationship with yourself and you share and create that with others. Valuing self is not an ego trip, narcissism or selfishness. It's understanding and experiencing what being divinely created truly means. Think about this: if you truly believe that you were created from an unknowable Greater Order and Direction, that you have a unique way of being that's different from everyone else because you have an important purpose to do in life, would you treat yourself like there's something wrong with you? Would you let others treat you like there's something wrong with you? Here's a short list of what valuing yourself can mean:

- you demonstrate liking and loving yourself through daily experiences
- you live a lifestyle of loving health and wellness
- you believe in abundance without greediness

- you love to support and serve others who ask for your help
- you make choices that support and grow the best of who you are
- you consciously choose love over fear
- you know how to say "YES" to life
- you only maintain *right relations* – healthy, loving, beneficial relationships
- you refuse to tolerate abuse in any form
- you say "NO" to toxic people and toxic relationships
- you expect to receive and make choices for validating experiences
- you take full responsibility for your actions and reactions
- you know that what you think, say, and do matters and impacts everyone and everything around you

Learning to value yourself is a life-long practice. Life is full of unexpected negative events that can disrupt our belief in the power of Love. When you are consciously practicing how to value yourself, you have the ability to transcend staying victimized by negative life experiences. This is mostly because when you are in the practice of valuing yourself, you easily and effortlessly attract the right people and resources to support your existence in a loving manner. No one can value you anymore or any less than how you value yourself.

## Emotional Barriers and Blocks to Be Overcome:

1. Isolation as Safety
2. Victim Consciousness
3. Scarcity Mentality

Isolation as Safety

Isolating yourself can be done even when you are surrounded by other people. It is how we withdraw ourselves from authentically and deeply engaging and interacting with others. Being a workaholic, where we choose to stay so busy that we don't tend to our authentic social needs, is a prime example of how we can isolate ourselves. Having only superficial relationships with colleagues or those we call friends, is another way in which we keep ourselves isolated.

Human beings are naturally social creatures. No one can achieve fulfillment in life all by themselves. To enable you to reach any of your goals, the Universe provides you with a network of people. These people play a variety of roles and make all sorts of contributions, both good and bad, to help you experience fulfillment and success. We all need the help of the right family members, friends, colleagues, and even acquaintances, and strangers. Having right relationships means that you will be vulnerable, and at times, you will experience the transference of pain. But deep, authentic connections are what enable you to heal and grow and learn to truly value yourself.

The other important reason why we need supportive people in our lives, is because one of the best ways to learn to value yourself is to make selfless contributions to the wellness, success and happiness of others. When someone gives you a sincere 'thank you' for your service, it lights you up inside because you are being told that you are aligned with your Higher Self. In other words, you're being told that you are divine.

Another really important reason for letting go of isolation in favor of authentic and loving relationships pertains to your journey towards self-mastery. You must be able and willing to receive truthful feedback. This is essential for learning self-mastery. When we are in the midst of a healing process, it is impossible to look at ourselves as objectively as another human being can. The best therapists and counselors are professionals who are skilled at providing supportive feedback that includes consideration of facts that you may have overlooked. Truth-telling is an essential part of all relationships, but especially those that involve intimacy. The true purpose of any intimate partnership is to have someone you love, and trust, give you honest feedback about how you are being with them, and with yourself.

Your trauma mind, encouraged by your pain body, may try to convince you that being alone or isolated will keep you safe from the pain of others. You know, that may sometimes be true, but it will never keep you safe from your own pain. You need a loving community to help you heal, grow and evolve.

## Victim Consciousness

Victim consciousness is the belief that you are your core wound or trauma. It is the belief that you are a victim to life, and there is never anything you can do about it. Usually this is hidden in your unconscious but can be evidenced by what you are experiencing in life. When you are living through victim consciousness, you attract people and situations that will make you right about being a victim. In other words, you will feel trapped in a world that is out to get you. Your best efforts will always be thwarted. Most unfortunate, is that you will begin to think that being a victim makes you better than other people. Believing that you are a victim to life, consciously or unconsciously, will not support you having your happy endings. You give your power away when you forget that you have the choice to not stay a victim or play the victim. Believing that you can never win is a sure way to never win!

The opposite of victim consciousness is victor consciousness. Instead of believing that you have to give your power away in order to be safe or just exist in the world, a victor conscious person owns their power and shares it. They don't need to have power over anyone or anything in order to feel safe and be happy. Living through victor consciousness is living the belief, 'the world is out to gift me!'

## Scarcity Mentality

Scarcity mentality is the belief in lack. It is a very detrimental belief system, especially for those who live in wealthy economies. Even when people are easily able to have their basic needs met, they will choose to focus on what is lacking in their lives. Scarcity mentality also creates the experiences of never allowing yourself to have enough. It is the fear that having fulfillment will not last. It is the fear that something bad will happen if you allow yourself to be fulfilled. People in scarcity mentality will always come up with excuses for why there isn't enough. They will also try to convince others that they are right.

This inability to experience what is enough is great evidence of the pain body being in charge of your life. Unhealed emotional pain will compel you to keep yourself busy with acquiring and accumulating. It's one of the best and easiest distractions that there is. It's the reason that on-line distributors like Amazon can be so successful. Your pain body will also keep you lacking because unconsciously you really don't believe you should have more. Either way, nothing will ever be enough until you can believe that it is.

Abundance mentality is the belief that everything you need in order to fulfill your dreams and higher purpose will come to you easily and effortlessly; and in the right way, at the right time. The main ingredients of abundance mentality are gratitude, patience, and faith. Not practicing these loving postures will keep fulfillment out of your reach, even when it has been achieved.

## Key #2 - CONTEMPLATION:

Please review and answer the following contemplative questions regarding the emotional barriers and blocks of the Earth Village internal landscape. This is not a quiz. There are no right or wrong answers. This is for you to discover what you need to discover about your emotional barriers and blocks.

1. What are 3 ways in which you value yourself?
2. What are 3 ways in which you don't value yourself?
3. How do people in your social circle, or with whom you hang out, demonstrate that they value you?
4. Are there people in your social circle, or with whom you hang out, who have shown that they don't value you? How have they shown you?
5. In what situations or circumstances do you feel like a victim, and why?
6. Where in your life do you believe that you are enough?
7. Where in your life do you believe you are lacking and are not enough?
8. What do you value most about yourself and your life?
9. Who do you value most in your life, and why?

# Key #3 - AFFIRMATION:

## Asking for Support with Valuing Self with Earth Ritual

*Great Mother. . .I'm tired of being a wanderer, I'm tired of giving that which I do not have. I'm tired of being told silently that this is all I can do. I want my real self to come out and to be seen. I want to go home. I want to be home. I want to be among people who see me for who I am, who make me feel as if I matter. Ashé!*
— from **The Healing Wisdom of Africa, by Malidoma Patrice Some, p.235**

### Step 1: Prepare a symbol of what needs to be healed

The element of Earth is the infinitely abundant home that we can rely upon to fulfill our every need. Earth energy has the ability to ground us, which is the state we must be in to receive abundance. Being grounded means we have remembered that we are supposed to be here, having our happy endings through purposeful living and loving support. Being grounded means you are willing to be on the path to move forward in life. We become ungrounded when we isolate ourselves, believe the we are victims to life, and either overindulge or deny ourselves because we are attached to scarcity mentality.

The Earth Element has the power to energetically pull out from you your barriers and blocks to abundance. This emptying out that you will experience will create new and open space for the more that is needed in your life. Right now, there is something new, something more that is wanting to enter your life. Right now, there are people waiting to meet you because it is to your mutual benefit regarding your higher purpose. The Earth element is a powerful ally to engage with for manifesting what you need to value yourself, and others.

Having done your contemplation of the three barriers and blocks to valuing yourself in the landscape of the Earth Village, it's time to prepare to make your faith gesture. For this ritual, you will decide what you want to manifest and prepare an offering, or reciprocity, for the Earth element in gratitude for the abundance energy she so generously shares. You'll begin by first calling on the Ancestors.

Ancestors can be called upon for all elemental rituals. For Earth rituals, calling specially on your female ancestors is very appropriate. Calling on the Ancestors for support is ancient tradition practiced by all indigenous cultures. The Dagara believe that the deceased leave this realm and return to the parallel world they call "The Land of the Ancestors." In that realm, the souls are no longer bound to their Earthly reality. They get to review their sacred contracts to learn if they kept all of their promises, and to integrate the lessons from their lifetime. Having had the experience of being in the physical realm, they become available as wisdom guides for those of us still Earth-bound. Their only hope is for us to not repeat their past wrongs, to win at being on purpose, and having our happy endings in life.

Once you have connected with your female ancestors, you will be ready to write out, draw some pictures, or fabricate some organic symbols of what you would like to manifest in your life to have conscious experiences of valuing of yourself, and others. By intending to value yourself, you will automatically be learning how to eliminate isolation, victim consciousness, and scarcity mentality. For example, if you are frustrated in your current job, you may want to manifest a new job where you are acknowledged, supported, and well compensated. If you are in a relationship that is emotionally and physically violent, you definitely want to manifest all the support you need to safely leave the situation. Whatever situation you might be in where you know you are giving your power away, choose to manifest experiences where you remember and are supported in your divine truth.

I highly recommend placing the writing, pictures, and/or symbols of what you would like to manifest on an Earth altar. Not only will this energetically support your faith gesture with the Earth element, it will also serve a visual reminder that you are manifesting the valuing of yourself. If you are unable to set up an altar, placing your manifestation request inside a box or a drawer where it will not be disturbed is also appropriate.

A very simple way to set up an Earth altar is to lay out a piece of yellow cloth on a table, counter or bureau, and place a safely burning yellow candle on it. Next, get some dirt (if you can get some from the place in which you were born, that would be wonderful) and place it in a small bowel or vessel. Holding the bowel or vessel of earth and saying a prayer of gratitude to the it will be very helpful. You may also place on your altar any other pictures or symbols of our beautiful Mother Earth.

The next part of the preparation process is making a bundle

that contains salt, sugar and white corn meal. You may create your bundle out of yellow cloth or yellow paper to honor the elemental color of Earth on the Dagara Medicine Wheel. The amount of salt, sugar and white corn meal you use is up to you. Since this is a ritual for abundance, I suggest making with as generous amounts as possible. The Dagara believe that Spirit loves beauty, and Mother Earth definitely appreciates receiving bundles that are pleasing to the eye. You may also garnish it with flowers.

Before you tie up your bundle, write out and include this affirmation request for your faith gesture:

> *Creator, All the One (however you address your God), enable me to receive your Grace for Valuing Myself and Others. Thank you, thank you, thank you.*

Placing your bundle on the Earth altar, or in a safe place until you are ready to do your ritual, will demonstrate that this bundle is sacred and worthy of respect.

## Step 2: Choosing and preparing right environment

Earth rituals must be performed outside in Nature. You will need to bury your offering in the Earth. Your faith gesture can be performed right in your own backyard, out in a wooded area, or forest. For those living in concrete-covered urban areas, if you are not able to find a patch of ground where you can legally bury your bundle, you may leave it by a tree or a rock in a city park. As with the Water ritual, you should find a spot that is off the beaten track and consider going at sunrise, or at a time that is safe with not many people around.

You can make a public outdoor space sacred through focus and intention. When you are focused and clear about your intention, people who notice you will respect your sacred space. A sacred space is a respected place that supports your willingness to go in and connect with your heart and soul. Everything you do in a sacred space is to be done with a sense of confidence, respect, patience and love. There is no need to rush through the process.

## Step 3: The Invocation

An invocation is a prayer and an invitation to your God, your Ancestors, Guardian Angels, Spirit guides, and Loving Entities to support you as you make your faith gesture through an elemental ritual. In calling forth the presence of the metaphysical, you are humbling yourself. You are admitting that you don't know how to transform your pain and that you need help. An invocation is also an expression of faith and gratitude for the help you need to receive. An invocation is most importantly said out loud as your vocal demonstration of your willingness to receive a healing grace. Here is an example of a simple invocation I have used before making a faith gesture using the element of Earth:

> *Creator, Mother-Father-God, Source, All-the-One, All That Is, I'm calling out to you to come and be with me right now, as I open myself to your greater Will. I thank you for my Ancestors, Spirit Guides, and Loving Entities, and knowing I cannot do this alone, I also call on them to assist me in pushing my ego aside, remaining humble, and allowing your healing energy to take hold of me. I also call upon the Spirit of Mother Earth and ask that she receive my bundle as a gift for her most generous abundance energy. Thank you, thank you, thank you for what I am about to receive, in the name of all that is Holy, I say Amen, Ashé, Ahau, Asa, Ashinga, Bismillah!*

There is no right or wrong way to do an invocation. Just

speak aloud from your heart, and let your soul do what it knows best -- to be loving.

## Step 4: Making the Faith Gesture

Once you've said your invocation, you are now ready to lovingly give over your bundle to Mother Earth. If weather and conditions permit, doing this ritual in bare feet is helpful. In bare feet, you will be grounded and even more open to receiving support for what you want to manifest.

Everyone's experience of making their faith gesture is unique. I've never in my almost 20 years of facilitating ritual have seen anyone do it the same way as anyone else. So, your experience of burying your bundle into the Earth, as a demonstration of your gratitude for support in learning to value yourself and others, cannot be dictated by me or anyone else. The Dagara believe that making this kind of an offering to the Earth enlivens it. With some much disregard of the Earth through nuclear testing and waste, and the removal of mountains for mining, your faith gesture is an honoring of the Earth. Also, you are allowing her to be of service to humanity in a very deep way. You may want to think about that as you are performing your ritual.

## Step 5: Gratitude and Closing

The final step in any elemental ritual is to take time to express gratitude. I always thank the element that has been my ally, as well as my Ancestors, all my Spirit Guides, and of course my God. I also take a moment to check for how I'm feeling emotionally. I usually feel glad, good, relieved, and free. To close out the ritual, you can take a drink of high vibrational water, like spring water.

**Note:** *At the very end of this chapter, you will find a link and code to a video on my website where I will acknowledge you for your work in the Earth Village and encourage you to continue on your Wisdom Walk to Self-Mastery healing journey.*

## Rewiring and Post-Ritual Care

The ancient technology of elemental ritual will have an effect on your mind, body and spirit. This healing process actually rewires your brain so that you can have access to new, positive, and generative thoughts and ideas. As old patterns of thoughts are being disrupted and revised, you may experience some or all of the following physical symptoms:

- very tired and needing to lay down and take naps
- wired, and not easily going to sleep or staying asleep
- very hungry all the time
- no appetite at all
- flu-like symptoms, including fever
- irrational sadness or laughing.

This list is not complete. They may be other unusual things that you experience.

Just remember that these are all "natural" results of the deep and important work you did on yourself. Rewiring usually last about 3-5 days, but it can last a little longer. Everyone is unique in how they experience their post-ritual process.

During your rewiring process, do be gentle and nurturing with yourself. Slow things down and allow yourself to get as much rest and relaxation as you can. Getting a massage, reiki, acupuncture, or other supports for your physical health, will be really good to do. Also, do drink lots of water to flush out the toxins that you are now able to shed out of your system. Once the symptoms pass, you will feel very well and open to learning and doing even more to support the transformation of your pain.

## Key #4 - REVELATION:

### Staying Awake to Insights & Clarity

Once you've progressed through your rewiring process, you will get validation that your faith gesture has made a difference in your life. It is usual to have awareness of a shift in how you are feeling, thinking, believing, and what you are doing. As I stated in the previous chapter regarding the Revelation Key, the gifts of greater knowledge and clarity about your true self will be unique. Sometimes they show up quietly in a dream, or through a conversation with someone you trust. Sometimes they hit you like a bolt of lightning. I suggest that you make note on a daily basis of what you are feeling, thinking, believing, and doing. By writing or recording what you are aware of, you will be growing your ability to be conscious of how *Valuing Yourself and Others* is removing barriers and blocks to your happy endings in life.

## Key #5 - SALVATION:

### The End of the Suffering

The Universe truly is always working on your behalf. You will know that the Grace of Valuing Yourself and Others has been given to you when what you have asked to manifest does so in ways you could never imagine! As I said before, the absence of suffering leaves your mind and emotions with the time and energy to create new experiences, new situations and more fulfilling relationships. All of that supports and grows your capacity for well-being, kindness, compassion, creativity, joy and love.

# CONGRATULATIONS!

You have used all 5 of your keys to self-mastery and left your village a much happier, healthier, and more loving place then when you arrived. It's now time to move forward and enter the Mineral Cave, where you will face the challenge of *Remembering Purpose*.

For a virtual acknowledgment of your progress, and encouragement for continuing your Wisdom Walk healing journey, click on the link below that will take you to my *Wisdom Walk to Self-Mastery* website. Once there, click on "Book Videos" and select the *Earth Ritual Praise*.

www.wisdomwalktoselfmastery.com

# Chapter 19

# The Mineral Cave

## Key #1 - MEDITATION:

*T*o support your willingness to transform your emotional pain, I ask at this point that you get still and meditate for at least 15 minutes. The meditative process helps you more easily access your inner landscape. I have recorded a meditation to specifically help you prepare for the inner work of this elemental landscape. Here's the link to my website www.wisdomwalktoselfmastery.com and Once there, click on "Book Videos" and select the *Mineral Cave Meditation.*

## Overview of the Elemental Landscape

The Mineral Cave is a symbol for the hidden, forgotten, or ignored aspect of our being human — our higher purpose in life. The Mineral Cave represents our internal domain which holds the knowledge of our higher purpose. It is here that you can find the many treasures you possess for living a meaningful and fulfilling life. This is the dwelling place of your genius -- which everyone has. Albert Einstein, the most famous scientific genius of the 20th century, has been tagged as saying that everyone has genius, but we lose sight of it when we think it should all look the same. Knowing that you were born with a unique genius to share with the world can make all the difference in how you choose to live your life.

As I discussed previously in this book, every human was born full of their truth. It is embedded in our bones, the Mineral essence of our human body. Our skeletal system of 270 bones contains a library of information and knowledge that is older than the Pyramids. The elemental force of Mineral enables us to connects with the right people, ideas, situations, and environments so we can enact our higher purpose. It is the job of parents and all adults in a community to help children remember their truth by observing, then supporting and validating that to which the child is naturally drawn. When this fails to happen, and purpose is dictated by parents, or schools, or gangs for the purpose of ego or financial security, then higher purpose goes into hiding.

Thankfully, our call to higher purpose never fully goes away. No matter how much success you may have in your business ventures and career, if you are not on purpose, you will not be at peace within your Self. Your achievements will never be enough to keep you happy. You will be feeling an emptiness inside, and you will seek to fill it with material things that can't last. By entering the inner landscape of your Mineral Cave, you will have the opportunity to clarify your calling and fill that emptiness with Love, which is eternal.

## The Healing Challenge: Remembering Purpose

Your higher purpose in life is why you matter to those around you, and why they matter to you. Remembering your purpose is a requirement for your experience of fulfillment and happy endings. When you are not living through purpose, you are either drifting through life or adopting a purpose that isn't yours. In either of these experiences, you will not find fulfillment.

Your higher purpose is your sacred contract. There are certain people you must meet, certain commitments you must keep, and certain sacrifices you must make. Even your body, and the manner in which it ages, has been specifically designed to serve your higher purpose. Unfortunately, most humans don't have this level of consciousness. Most people will go through their whole lives unaware of how much they matter because they have never taken the time to remember and clarify their true purpose for living.

The lead character in the classic Christmas movie from 1946, *It's a Wonderful Life,* is a perfect example of how you can live most of your life unaware of your higher purpose. George Bailey, the lead character, wanted to travel around the world and build things. Those dreams were thwarted by family and life circumstances. George felt obligated to pick up his father's legacy, but he did not believe that his work at the Building & Loan Company was as significant or big as building a bridge or a skyscraper. Finally, with the help of a financial crisis, George was able to realize that everything that he did in his life was for a higher purpose. Not only did he save the life of his brother and keep the local pharmacist from accidentally poisoning someone and going to jail, Georg was the bulwark against the greed and mean-spiritedness of his business rival, Mr. Potter. If it weren't for George's commitment to the well-being of others, Potter would have turned hometown Bedford Falls into a pit of vice and violence.

When you become willing and able to remember your higher purpose, and to allow it to be your navigator through the journey of life, everything that happens to you will be quite meaningful. Purposeful living enables you to ultimately experience and understand everything that happens to you as a blessing – regardless of what form it takes. When you remember how much your life really matters, how you are so not disposable, you will consistently experience your happy endings.

# Emotional Barriers and Blocks to Be Overcome

1. Comparing Yourself to Others
2. People Pleasing
3. Being Who You Are Not

## Comparing Yourself to Others

Being the unique individual that you are, when you compare yourself to another person, you will always come up short. There is only one 'you' and measuring yourself against someone you are not will always bring suffering. Even if you are in a competition, and you become the winner, you are only a winner as long as someone else is a loser. In other words, you are attached to what someone else doesn't do in order to be your best, instead of knowing that you are enough, and people can love you exactly the way you are. The biggest challenge for anyone involved in a competition is to love themselves if they don't make it to the number one spot.

As children, especially for the first ten years, we do learn by comparison. As we enter adulthood we have been inspired by or learned from what other people do, have, or say. But, comparing yourself is an awful waste of time and energy. Unfortunately, our Western consumer culture that is taking over the world, uses comparison and judgement to market and advertise. We are constantly told through television, radio, magazines, social media, billboards and everywhere an advertisement can be inserted, that we are not enough but using a certain product will make us all right. These daily doses of invalidation make it challenging to believe that your uniqueness is the key to knowing and living your higher purpose.

## People Pleasing

People pleasing is not just about being willing to cooperate with and support others with what they need. It's about doing that to the exclusion and/or detriment of your own needs. When you 'people please', you are making a one-way bargain to get what you want by going along with someone else's program. One-way bargains mean that you do not have the agreement of the other person or persons that they will also go along with your program. This form of bargaining always fails.

People pleasing is rooted in low or absent self-esteem. It's another form of giving your power away because you don't believe you can have what you need any other way. People pleasing is a huge distraction to self-mastery and having your happy endings because you spend time doing for others what you could be doing for yourself. When you believe that you can't be liked, loved, or supported for who you are, then you will manipulate what you do in order to get attention and approval. Being manipulative means you are not being your authentic self. Without authenticity, you cannot live your higher purpose.

## Being Who-You-Are-Not

When you live your life as a people pleaser, easily you become someone that isn't truly you. As a result, the who-you-are-not will become more real to you than your authentic self. Being who-you-are-not may give you a sense of safety and security. You will be doing what you believe makes you a good and right person. You may have homes, cars, and free flowing income to prove to yourself that you are a success, which has to mean that you are living your truth. From this perspective, it is understandable that when your higher purpose comes calling, you don't want to answer the door.

Answering the call to higher purpose, stepping onto the path to your authentic self will be disruptive to whatever lifestyle you are living. It can cause the breakup of relationships, resignations from jobs, loss of a wealthy lifestyle, and the questioning of your sanity by others, and even yourself. Still, the ever-present energy of self-love and inner peace that you experience when living your higher purpose makes whatever disruption you had to go through totally worth it. It is important to accept what all successful people know: money and prestige cannot tell you your higher purpose, or the truth of who you are.

I do believe that most humans have to experience who they are not so that they can become who they are. Becoming your authentic self is a growing process. At some point, something inside of you will tell you that there is something you are missing. The longer you live, being who-you-are-not will become more and more of an emotional and even physical burden.

## Key #2 - CONTEMPLATION:

Please review and answer the following contemplative questions regarding the emotional barriers and blocks of internal landscape of the Mineral Cave. This is not a quiz. There are no right or wrong answers. This is for you to discover what you need to discover about your emotional barriers and blocks.

1. Who is the person or persons you most compared yourself to when you were growing up? Do you still compare yourself to them?
2. Who in your current circle of family and friends compares themselves to you? Why do you think they do so?
3. What is the one thing you really want to change about yourself, and why?
4. Who do you find yourself 'people pleasing' most of the time and why? How does this behavior serve you?
5. Who do you really think you are?

6. Who do you think people really think you are?
7. What is your biggest challenge to being your authentic self?
8. What would support you in being fully your authentic self?
9. What have you felt called to do in life?
10. What do you think is your higher purpose and why?

# Key #3 - AFFIRMATION:

## Asking for Support with Remembering Purpose

*Mineral rituals aim at restoring lost memories...Mineral tells us that we know what we need to know, if we would but remember. The elders say that the rocks can speak, but their voice is so tiny that it can barely be heard. The rocks remind us to be still and to listen carefully, to stop searching outside of ourselves for that which we already hold within.*
— **from The Healing Wisdom of Africa, by Malidoma Patrice Some, pp.243,256**

### Step 1: Prepare a symbol of what needs to be healed

The element of Mineral is an incredibly powerful ally for remembering and clarifying your higher purpose. Minerals include rocks, stones, crystals, precious metals, bones, shells, and sand, which is pulverized stone. Mountains, hills, and caves are also part of the Mineral family and are referred to by many indigenous cultures as *the bones of the Earth*. For centuries, humans from every culture have used crystals, such as quartz, amethyst, agate and obsidian, for psychic, emotional and physical healing. Like the dirt beneath our feet, minerals are abundant and all around us. Even urban dwellers can't escape them. Concrete and high rises all contain stones.

Minerals can be powerful conductors of energy waves. Chips of clear quartz crystal are used in modern communication technology like cell phones and computers. Minerals are great recordkeepers and storytellers. Ask any geologist who does research at sacred sites like the Grand Canyon or the Great Pyramids of Giza. The manner in which the stones have corroded over time tell the story of how the Earth was formed and how it evolved. The opportunity to engage with the Mineral element for remembering and receiving validation of our higher purpose is a most wonderful gift from God and the Universe.

Having done your contemplation of the three barriers and blocks to remembering purpose in the landscape of the Mineral Cave, it's time to prepare to make your faith gesture. This ritual can be done in the complete privacy of your home, or you may choose to go out into Nature. Whether you use crystals or stones you already have in your possession, or you go out and buy some, or you go to a natural setting where you are surrounded by stones, you will be asking and allowing the Minerals to speak to you. As with every elemental ritual, you'll begin by first calling on the Ancestors.

Calling on the Ancestors for support is an ancient tradition practiced by all indigenous cultures. The Dagara believe that the deceased leave this realm and return to the parallel world they call "The Land of the Ancestors." In that realm, the souls are no longer bound to their Earthly reality. They get to review their sacred contracts to learn if they kept all of their promises, and to integrate the lessons from their lifetime. Having had the experience of being in the physical realm, they become available as wisdom guides for those of us still Earth-bound. Their only hope is for us to not repeat their past wrongs, to win at being on purpose, and having our happy endings in life.

Once you have connected with your ancestors, I strongly

suggest making a Mineral altar. A very simple way to set up Mineral altar is to lay out a piece of white cloth on a table, counter or bureau, and place a safely burning white candle on it. Next, get some stones, crystals, shells or bones that have meaning for you. If you need and choose to purchase some crystals, be sure to include clear quartz, because it transmits the energy of clarity. Once you have your minerals, arrange them on your altar in a manner that is intuitive and beautiful to you. You may also place pictures of mountains, caves, or sacred mineral places like Stonehenge, Machu Picchu, or the Great Pyramids of Giza. If you are unable to set up an altar, place some minerals in your pockets or wear them on you. Consciously wearing jewelry that has crystals or precious gems is another wonderful way to connect with the Mineral element.

What's most important in working with minerals, is that you take them seriously and treat them like they are alive and precious. This is the reciprocity for them serving you. Minerals have so much knowledge and wisdom to share, but not many people consciously call upon them for help. So, your asking for their help automatically means that you will receive it. They love being used in this way. Take time to hold them carefully and intend to feel something energetically. Express your gratitude for them as you notice their shapes, their colors and designs. Often you can see miniature pictures of faces or animals embedded. Sometimes you can even see miniature landscapes and towns. Minerals are always wanting and happy to share their stories.

Now, with your minerals in place, you are now ready to write out, draw some pictures, or fabricate some organic symbols of what you have identified as your blocks and barriers to remembering your higher purpose. You will place your writing and/or symbols on your altar. If you aren't able to create the altar, then put them in a safe space where they won't be disturbed while you are making your faith gesture. Place some minerals in that space as well to help keep everything connected.

Last, but not least, write out this affirmation request for your faith gesture and also place it on your Mineral altar or safe space:

> *Creator, All the One (however you address your God), enable me to receive your Grace for Remembering and Receiving Clarity about my Higher Purpose in life. Thank you, thank you, thank you!*

## Step 2: Choosing and preparing right environment

Mineral rituals are ideally performed out in Nature. I had the wonderful opportunity to live in the Smoky Mountains, which is an incredible Mineral Kingdom. I could easily find large configurations of rocks and boulders and did many Mineral rituals. If you are unable to access a Mineral Kingdom, your faith gesture can be performed right in your own backyard, or inside your home. As long as you are close to your Mineral altar and/or pocketing and wearing your minerals, you will be able to communicate with them. You may also want to have a notebook or paper and pen to write down what they communicate to you.

To invoke the sacred in your outdoor or indoor space, again use focus and intention. A sacred space is a respected place that supports your willingness to go in and connect with your heart and soul. Everything you do in a sacred space is to be done with a sense of confidence, respect, patience and love. There is no need to rush through the process.

## Step 3: The Invocation

An invocation is a prayer and an invitation to your God, your Ancestors, Guardian Angels, spirit guides, and loving entities to support you as you make your faith gesture through an elemental ritual. In calling forth the presence of the metaphysical, you are humbling yourself. You are admitting that you don't know how to transform your pain and that you need help. An invocation is also an expression of faith and gratitude for the help you need to receive. An invocation is most importantly said out loud as your vocal demonstration of your willingness to receive a healing grace. Here is an example of a simple invocation I have used before making a faith gesture using the element of Mineral:

> *Creator, Mother-Father-God, Source, All-the-One, All That Is, I'm calling out to you to come and be with me right now, as I open myself to your greater Will. I thank you for my Ancestors, Spirit Guides, and Loving Entities, and knowing I cannot do this alone, I also call on them to assist me in pushing my ego aside, remaining humble, and allowing your healing energy to take hold of me. I also call upon the Spirit of the Minerals and ask that they hear and respond to my request for help with remembering my higher purpose. Thank you, thank you, thank you for what I am about to receive, in the name of all that is Holy, I say Amen, Ashé, Ahau, Asa, Ashinga, Bismillah!*

There is no right or wrong way to do an invocation. Just speak aloud from your heart, and let your soul do what it knows best – to be loving.

**Step 4: Making the Faith Gesture**

Once you've said your invocation, you are now ready to work with the Mineral element. It helps to open your mind to memories that can be guide posts to your higher purpose, as this will signal the Minerals that you are open to receive their information for you. In a very relaxed state, sitting or lying down, close your eyes and think about a time in your life when you were doing something you really liked to do, and you felt useful. This should not be a time when you were doing something harmful to yourself or others, or something that would have bad consequences.

Once you have that memory, relive it in your mind not only experiencing what it looked like, but what it felt like emotionally and physically. Next, ask the Minerals to bring you more memories of when you were doing something you liked and also felt useful. In this somewhat meditative state, ask the Minerals for clarity about your higher purpose. Allow them to channel their messages to you without doubt or disruption. Have your pen and paper or voice recorder nearby if necessary.

Everyone's experience of making their faith gesture is unique. I've never in my almost 20 years of facilitating ritual have seen anyone do it the same way as anyone else. So, your experience of communicating with the Mineral Spirits to remember your higher purpose cannot be dictated by me or anyone else. If you do not receive any messages from them during the time you spend in ritual, know that the messages will come to you, usually within three days. The messages can show up in your dreams, through a conversation you have, through a movie your watch, a song you hear, or in a book you read, or even on a billboard. Stay awake to receiving what you need to know in any and every form possible. Continue to keep your symbols of your blocks and barriers to remembering purpose on your altar or in a safe place until you feel that you have received your Mineral messages.

## Step 5: Gratitude and Closing

The final step in any elemental ritual is to take time to express gratitude. I always thank the element that has been my ally, as well as my Ancestors, all my spirit guides, and of course my God. I also take a moment to check for how I'm feeling emotionally. I usually feel glad, good, relieved, and free. To close out the ritual, you can touch the stones, bones, crystals and shells you worked with, saying 'thank you' out loud. The symbols of your blocks and barriers can be kept on your Mineral altar or in a safe space as a reminder that you are no longer willing to compare yourself to others, to people please, or let go of your authentic self.

**Note:** *At the very end of this chapter, you will find a link and code to a video on my website where I will acknowledge you for your work in the inner landscape of the Mineral Cave and encourage you to continue on your Wisdom Walk healing journey.*

## Rewiring and Post-Ritual Care

The ancient technology of elemental ritual will have an effect on your mind, body and spirit. This healing process actually rewires your brain so that you can have access to new, positive, and generative thoughts and ideas. As old patterns of thoughts are being disrupted and revised, you may experience some or all of the following physical symptoms:

- very tired and needing to lay down and take naps
- wired, and not easily going to sleep or staying asleep
- very hungry all the time
- no appetite at all
- flu-like symptoms, including fever
- irrational sadness or laughing.

This list is not complete. They may be other unusual things that you experience.

Just remember that these are all "natural" results of the deep and important work you did on yourself. Rewiring usually last about 3-5 days, but it can last a little longer. Everyone is unique in how they experience their post-ritual process.

During your rewiring process, do be gentle and nurturing with yourself. Slow things down and allow yourself to get as much rest and relaxation as you can. Getting a massage, reiki, acupuncture, or other supports for your physical health, will be really good to do. Also, do drink lots of water to flush out the toxins that you are now able to shed out of your system. Once the symptoms pass, you will feel very well and open to learning and doing even more to support the transformation of your pain.

# Key #4 - REVELATION:

## Staying Awake to Insights & Clarity

Once you've progressed through your rewiring process, you will get validation that your faith gesture has made a difference in your life. It is usual to have awareness of a shift in how you are feeling, thinking, believing, and what you are doing. As I stated in the previous chapter regarding the Revelation Key, the gifts of greater knowledge and clarity about your true self will be unique. Sometimes they show up quietly in a dream, or through a conversation with someone you trust. Sometimes they hit you like a bolt of lightning. I suggest that you make note on a daily basis of what you are feeling, thinking, believing, and doing. By writing or recording what you are aware of, you will be growing your ability to be conscious of how *Remembering Purpose* is removing barriers and blocks to your happy endings in life.

# Key #5 - SALVATION:

## The End of the Suffering

The Universe truly is always working on your behalf. You will know that the Grace of Remembering Your Higher Purpose has been given to you when what you have asked to manifest does so in ways you could never imagine! As I said before, the absence of suffering leaves your mind and emotions with the time and energy to create new experiences, new situations and better relationships. All of that supports and grows your capacity for well-being, kindness, compassion, creativity, joy and love.

# CONGRATULATIONS!

You have used all 5 of your keys to self-mastery and discovered some treasure of the truth of who you are. You are now prepared to enter the Land of Nature and face the challenge of *Welcoming Change*.

For a virtual acknowledgment of your progress, and encouragement for continuing your Wisdom Walk healing journey, click on the link below that will take you to my *Wisdom Walk to Self-Mastery* website. Once there, click on "Book Videos" to access the *Mineral Ritual Praise*.

www.wisdomwalktoselfmastery.com

# Chapter 20

# The Land of Nature

## Key #1 - MEDITATION:

*T*o support your willingness to transform your emotional pain, I ask at this point that you get still and meditate for at least 15 minutes. The meditative process helps you more easily access your inner landscape. I have recorded a meditation to specifically help you prepare for the inner work of this elemental landscape. Here's the link to my website www.wisdomwalktoselfmastery.com

Once there, click on "Book Videos" to access the *Land of Nature Meditation.*

## Overview of the Elemental Landscape

The Land of Nature is the fifth and final internal landscape of the *Wisdom Walk to Self-Mastery* healing journey. It is the result of all the work that you have done on yourself in the four previous landscapes. The Land of Nature symbolizes your human evolutionary impulse, your natural ability to become the best version of your Self.

You are divinely wired for healing, growth, and evolution. Despite this natural impulse, you, me and all humans are challenged by change. We don't normally like it because it disrupts our comfort zone, that place where we believe we know what is happening, and what will be happening. Not knowing what is or will be happening makes us feel very vulnerable, and change throws us head first into 'not knowing'.

Without change, though, we will never experience the grace of forgiveness, the power of peacemaking, how valuable we truly are, or the joy of our higher purpose.

The nature of change is that it is messy. It always brings things you didn't expect or plan on, even when you have known that the change was coming. Along with being made vulnerable, the messiness of change is why we so resist it. Unexpected change is one of the most emotionally challenging experiences anyone can ever go through, like the sudden death of a loved one, or the unexpected loss of a job. Despite these and other painful upsets, change always brings us gifts. There is something inside you that truly knows this. To resist change is painful and futile. This is an essential component of how the Universe works. So learning how to welcome change and even embrace it is how we can more easily access the gifts it brings.

## The Healing Challenge: Welcoming Change

The great 13th century Sufi poet and mystic, Rumi, wrote a poem that is called *Guest House*. It is one of the most frequently shared and quoted of his poems in modern times. Rumi, through his poem, reminds us that change is inevitable and therefore must have a purpose:

> *This being human is a guest house.*
> *Every morning a new arrival.*
>
> *A joy, a depression, meanness,*
> *Some momentary awareness comes*
> *As an unexpected visitor.*
>
> *Welcome and attend them all!*
> *Even if they're a crowd of sorrows,*

*Who violently sweep your house*
*Empty of its furniture,*
*Still treat each guest honorably.*

*He may be clearing you out*
*For some new delight.*

*The dark thought, the shame, the malice,*
*Meet them at the door laughing,*
*And invite them in.*

*Be grateful for whoever comes,*
*Because each has been sent*
*As a guide from beyond.*

*Welcome difficulty.*
*Learn the alchemy True Human Beings know:*
*The moment you accept what troubles*
*You've been given, the door opens.*

*Welcome difficulty as a familiar comrade.*
*Joke with torment brought by the Friend.*

*Sorrows are the rage of old clothes*
*And jackets that serve to cover,*
*And then are taken off.*
*That undressing and the beautiful*
*Naked body underneath,*
*Is the sweetness that comes after grief.*

The idea of welcoming change has clearly been around for a very long time. Yet, we find this so very hard to do. It doesn't seem to make sense to our rational minds. We think, how can a loss, a betrayal, an eviction, or any painful experience be ultimately designed to grow and evolve us towards happy endings in life? The truth is, I don't know of anyone, including myself, who hasn't had to go through something challenging by which you are stretched and grown. That stretching and growing process is a universal requirement for becoming the more of who you are, so you can experience your higher purpose.

As human beings, we can learn to consciously welcome all change, whether it is winning a 25-million-dollar lottery or being betrayed by someone we loved and trusted. We can learn to let go of our resistance and open ourselves up to discover how the change is a benefit. Instead of trying to know, we can remain curious and open to learning. We can learn to choose love for ourselves over fear from our change. Welcoming changes takes a lot of courage and practice. It doesn't come easily. However, just being willing to learn how to do it will enable you to remember the truth: *that in the midst of your fear and upset, there is always purpose and treasure awaiting.*

## Emotional Barriers and Blocks to Be Overcome

1. Avoidance
2. Attachment to the Past
3. Self-Sabotage

### Avoidance

One of the most common ways to resist change is to simply avoid it. Even when it is happening all around you, you can choose to ignore it and make up excuses for why everything should or will stay the same. Sometimes when change shows up, rather than accept it, we will look for someone to blame for the upsets, disturbances and chaos that accompanies new things coming into our life. Blaming someone, even God, may create some distraction and buy you some time, but eventually you will have to deal with the change.

Avoiding change will not make it go away. It will only cause the Universe to bring you more frequent and radical wake-up calls or smack-downs to get your attention. I'm sure you know of someone, possibly yourself, who was in situation that was changing but who chose to ignore the evidence. Instead of welcoming the change and taking on the work of preparing for the next steps, they waited until there was nothing they could do anymore but go along with the change. Instead of walking with their head held high, excited for the new adventures that awaited them, they felt victimized, they blamed and complained, and transferred their pain. In the automotive business world, this is what happened to the Detroit automakers. The citizens of Detroit and other surrounding areas are still bearing the consequences.

In the late 1960s and early 1970s when Japan introduced smaller, more fuel efficient, and less expensive cars to the US market, young buyers embraced them. The big three -- Ford, General Motors, and Chrysler, ignored this huge sign of change at a time when young people were concerned about the impact of carbon dioxide on the ecology. They didn't take the Japanese cars seriously. They thought it was just a fad.

Within 10 years, the Toyota Camry became the biggest selling car in America, and the auto industry in and around Detroit began a slow and steady decline, creating one of the most tragic regional economic collapses in the history of the United States. President Barack Obama, backed by the US Senate and Congress, had to give them a federal bailout to avoid bankruptcy in 2009 through 2013. If only they could have welcomed the change to their industry, much of the unemployment and the social ills that accompany it could have been avoided.

## Attachment to The Past

Holding on to our past, to the way things have always been, seems like a good thing to do. As humans, we seem to naturally latch on to what we believe and understand in the face of something new and different. When the leaders of the 17th century Catholic Church of Rome were told by the science pioneer, Galileo Galilei, that the Sun, and not the Earth, was the center of the planetary system, he was tried in a court, labelled a heretic, and placed on house arrest for nine years until his death. The religious authorities totally resisted the idea of what we now have photographically proven to be our solar system.

Change and evolutionary realities cause a domino effect. They put you in a position to have to question, rethink, and at times, unlearn what you thought you knew was right. Being right makes you feel more confident about yourself and your world. Nobody enjoys not knowing the right answer. Of course, staying attached to what you believe and the plans you've made in the face of change will not end well. Letting go of our attachment to knowing and having to be right can open our minds to learning the truth. When we step into curiosity about our life and what is happening in the present moment, we can more easily and effortlessly reach our happy endings and fulfillment in life.

## Self-Sabotage

In the Walt Disney animated version of Alice's journey through Wonderland, there is a wonderful demonstration of what self-sabotaging your growth and change could look like. As I remember it, Alice comes through a doorway into a dark room that has only a table, and nothing else. On the table is a little medicine bottle with a sign attached that says, "Drink Me!" So Alice drinks the contents of the bottle and grows to a *ginormous* size. There's a moment when she is so uncomfortable with her growth that she wished she could squeeze back through what is now the size of a mouse hole and return to where she was before.

This is self-sabotage. Unbeknownst to Alice, her new size and what lies ahead on her journey is exactly what she needs for finding her way back home. We are no different from Alice when our new and different experiences show up. Although we will have outgrown our past and evolved to a next level of who we are, at first, we will long for the comfort of what we knew. Having to face the unknown that our new growth presents is just plain scary!

Please know that self-sabotage doesn't begin in a conscious way. No one wakes up in the morning determined not to have their blessings and good fortune. So, you usually don't become aware that you are blocking and resisting your happy endings until you feel the sting and pain of trying to squeeze back through the hole (your past). The cosmic law of change, which includes healing, growth and evolution, is that there is no going back! This means, that even if you return to the dysfunctional relationship, the unfulfilling job, or the experience of a prison cell, and you've become more conscious of the truth of who you are, you will not be at peace. There really is no going back.

## Key #2 - CONTEMPLATION:

Please review and answer the following contemplative questions regarding the emotional barriers and blocks of internal landscape of the Land of Nature. This is not a quiz. There are no right or wrong answers. This is for you to discover what you need to discover about your emotional barriers and blocks.

1. What was the most beneficial change you ever experienced in your life?

2. What was the hardest change you ever experienced in your life?
3. What has been your pattern for resisting change? Do you avoid it, ignore it, disregard it, or play the blame game?
4. Think of a time when you sabotaged moving forward from your past. What were the consequences of your self-sabotage?
5. How challenging is it for you when:
   a. change has left you not knowing what's next
   b. you find out that you were wrong about what you thought you knew
   c. you are challenged by someone else's opinion
6. When were you most able to welcome change coming into your life? What supported you to be able to do that?
7. When were you not able to welcome change into your life? Of what were you most afraid?
8. What has shifted and changed for you since your last birthday?
9. At this time in your life, what would you like to change?
10. As you consider change coming into your life in the future, what do you anticipate and what do you fear?

# Key #3 - AFFIRMATION:

## Asking for Support with Welcoming Change

*Nature rituals, like mineral rituals, help people remain focused on their true purpose. To be human is to be engaged in a challenging task of continual readjustment and fine-tuning, especially in a world that struggles to distance itself from nature. The repeated distractions that plague life in the modern*

*world separate us not only from the natural world but from our own essential nature.*
— from **The Healing Wisdom of Africa, by Malidoma Patrice Some, pp.243,256**

### Step 1: Prepare a symbol of what needs to be healed

The element of Nature provides the greatest example for humans of the necessity of change. Nature shows how essential change is for all living things, and the profound beauty that can be seen and felt as a result of change. I'm talking of course about the change in the seasons, and the change in the weather. Nobody loves the extreme cold of the winter, but when spring arrives it makes the season of ice and cold so worth it. Nobody likes tornadoes or hurricanes, but despite the destruction they can leave in their wake, the sky never looks bluer or sunnier after the storm has passed. It's like a message from Nature that we can rebuild and be reborn.

Nature as the culmination of the other four elements, has the energetic ability to help us manifest more than just materials things. With its knowledge of the cycle of life, death and rebirth, it can magically remove what's no longer of service to our well-being and open us up to receive the new that we need. The element of Nature can support our ability to release the past, stay curious (not knowing) about the future, and embrace the present. In this manner, we are more able to welcome the necessary changes that will bring us our happy endings – easily and effortlessly.

Having done your contemplation of the three barriers and blocks to *Welcoming Change* in the landscape of the Nature element, it's time to prepare to make your faith gesture. Like the Earth ritual, a Nature ritual has to be done outside in nature.

As with every elemental ritual, you'll begin by first calling on the Ancestors.

Calling on the Ancestors for support is an ancient tradition practiced by all indigenous cultures. The Dagara believe that the deceased leave this realm and return to the parallel world they call "The Land of the Ancestors." In that realm, the souls are no longer bound to their Earthly reality. They get to review their sacred contracts to learn if they kept all of their promises, and to integrate the lessons from their lifetime. Having had the experience of being in the physical realm, they become available as wisdom guides for those of us still Earth-bound. Their only hope is for us to not repeat their past wrongs, to win at being on purpose, and having our happy endings in life.

Once you have connected with your ancestors, I strongly suggest making a Nature altar. A very simple way to set up Nature altar is to lay out a piece of green cloth on a table, counter or bureau, and place a safely burning green candle on it. Once you've laid out the foundation, place any and all representations of the Nature element. This includes flowers, plants, something made out of wood, some twigs or pieces of bark shed from a tree, animal figurines, animals skins, pictures of plants, trees, animals, humans, and a nature scene. Be creative and remember Spirit loves beauty.

If you are unable to set up an altar, place some of the above items in a drawer, a box, or any safe space where they won't be disturbed.

Once you've set up your Nature altar or placed your symbols of Nature in a safe place, you will be ready to make lists, draw some pictures, or fabricate some organic symbols of what you believe are your barriers or blocks to welcoming change. However, you decide to create the symbols of what needs transforming, know that you will be putting them into a bundle. The Dagara believe that Spirit loves beauty, and Nature spirits definitely appreciate receiving bundles that are pleasing to the eye. So, make your bundles out of lovely-looking wrapping paper or cloth. You may also garnish it with flowers. When in doubt about what paper or cloth to use, know that both all shades of green are appropriate, as this is the color associated with the Nature element in the Dagara Medicine Wheel.

Before you tie up your bundle, write out and include this affirmation request for your faith gesture:

> *Creator, All the One (however you address your God),*
> *enable me to receive your Grace for Welcoming Change*
> *into my life. Thank you, thank you, thank you.*

Place your bundle on your Nature altar or in your safe space until you are ready to take it out into Nature and release it.

## Step 2: Choosing and preparing right environment

A Nature ritual is a wonderful opportunity to walk through a forest, hike a trail, or stroll through a city park as you open yourself up to spirit and messages from the Nature elements. For some of you, staying right in your own backyard will work, as long as it gives you access to trees, plants, flowers, butterflies, beetles, and wild animals such as birds, squirrels, chipmunks, rabbits, snakes, or any other animals that dwell in proximity to humans.

It will be important to pay attention to the animals and trees that you encounter during your time in Nature. For thousands of years, humans have observed and created myths and assigned symbols to both animals and trees. A noted shamanic Wisdomkeeper and storyteller, Ted Andrews, wrote the quintessential books on what our allies in Nature symbolize. I highly recommend these books for learning about the messages from nature: *Animal-Speak, Animal-Wise,* and *Nature-Speak.* You can also use Google to look up animal and tree totem information. Knowing the symbolic messages of the animals and trees will make your Nature ritual even more meaningful. Of course, you may receive messages directly from the animals and trees that you will encounter.

To invoke the sacred in your outdoor space, again use focus and intention. A sacred space is a respected place that supports your willingness to go in and connect with your heart and soul. Everything you do in a sacred space is to be done with a sense of confidence, respect, patience and love. There is no need to rush through the process.

### Step 3: The Invocation

An invocation is a prayer and an invitation to your God, your Ancestors, Guardian Angels, spirit guides, and loving entities to support you as you make your faith gesture through an elemental ritual. In calling forth the presence of the metaphysical, you are humbling yourself. You are admitting that you don't know how to transform your pain and that you need help. An invocation is also an expression of faith and gratitude for the help you need to receive. An invocation is most importantly said out loud as your vocal demonstration of your willingness to receive a healing grace. Here is an example of a simple invocation I have used before making a faith gesture using the element of Mineral:

> *Creator, Mother-Father-God, Source, All-the-One, All That Is, I'm calling out to you to come and be with me right now, as I open myself to your greater Will. I thank you for my Ancestors, Spirit Guides, and Loving Entities, and knowing I cannot do this alone, I also call on them to assist me in pushing my ego aside, remaining humble, and allowing your healing energy to take hold of me. I also call upon the Nature Spirits and ask that they hear and respond to my request for releasing my resistance to Welcoming Change. Thank you, thank you, thank you for what I am about to receive, in the name of all that is Holy, I say Amen, Ashé, Ahau, Asa, Ashinga, Bismillah!*

There is no right or wrong way to do an invocation. Just speak aloud from your heart, and let your soul do what it knows best – to be loving.

### Step 4: Making the Faith Gesture

Once you've said your invocation, you are now ready to work with the Nature element. Remember to bring your bundle along with you. You will be exploring your natural landscape ritualistically, meaning you will trust that everything that happens, everything that shows up is designed to support your healing process.

You can connect with Nature in a variety of ways. You can just meander through your locale and pay close attention to any animal that shows up as you walk. You can ask and thank it for sharing any message or messages it may have for you. As with the minerals, allow them to channel their messages to you without doubt or disruption. Have your pen and paper or voice recorder nearby if necessary.

Another way to connect with Nature is to find a tree that calls to you and sit by it or up against it if you can. Stay sitting or observing with the tree long enough to experience a communion with it. Yes, trees can also talk! We just have to be open and be willing to listen with our heart and soul.

At some point in your Nature journey, you will be called to release your bundle. When you feel it is the right time and discover the right place, express out loud what it is that you want to change in your life at this time. Express gratitude again to the Nature spirits for their willingness to transform your resistance to this needed change.

Everyone's experience of making their faith gesture is unique. I've never in my almost 20 years of facilitating ritual have seen anyone do it the same way as anyone else. So, your experience of communicating with the Nature Spirits to welcome change cannot be dictated by me or anyone else. If you do not receive any direct messages during the time you spend in ritual, know that the messages will come to you, usually within three days. The messages can show up in your dreams, through a conversation you have, through a movie your watch, a song you hear, or in a book you read, or even on a billboard. Stay awake to receiving what you need to know in any and every form possible. Also, look up the symbolic/ totem meaning for any animals and trees you connected with along your journey.

## Step 5: Gratitude and Closing

The final step in any elemental ritual is to take time to express gratitude. I always thank the element that has been my ally, as well as my Ancestors, all my Spirit Guides, and of course my God. I also take a moment to check for how I'm feeling emotionally. I usually feel glad, good, relieved, and free. To close out the ritual, you can touch or hug a tree, saying 'thank you' out loud.

**Note:** *At the very end of this chapter, you will find a link and code to a video on my website where I will acknowledge you for your work in the inner landscape of the Land of Nature and a congratulation for completing your Wisdom Walk to Self-Mastery healing journey.*

## Rewiring and Post-Ritual Care

The ancient technology of elemental ritual will have an effect on your mind, body and spirit. This healing process actually rewires your brain so that you can have access to new, positive, and generative thoughts and ideas. As old patterns of thoughts are being disrupted and revised, you may experience some or all of the following physical symptoms:

- very tired and needing to lay down and take naps

- wired, and not easily going to sleep or staying asleep
- very hungry all the time
- no appetite at all
- flu-like symptoms, including fever
- irrational sadness or laughing.

This list is not complete. They may be other unusual things that you experience.

Just remember that these are all "natural" results of the deep and important work you did on yourself. Rewiring usually last about 3-5 days, but it can last a little longer. Everyone is unique in how they experience their post-ritual process.

During your rewiring process, do be gentle and nurturing with yourself. Slow things down and allow yourself to get as much rest and relaxation as you can. Getting a massage, reiki, acupuncture, or other supports for your physical health, will be really good to do. Also, do drink lots of water to flush out the toxins that you are now able to shed out of your system. Once the symptoms pass, you will feel very well and open to learning and doing even more to support the transformation of your pain.

# Key #4 - REVELATION:

### Staying Awake to Insights & Clarity

Once you've progressed through your rewiring process, you will get validation that your faith gesture has made a difference in your life. It is usual to have awareness of a shift in how you are feeling, thinking, believing, and what you are doing. As I stated in the previous chapter regarding the Revelation Key, the gifts of greater knowledge and clarity about your true self will be unique. Sometimes they show up quietly in a dream, or through a conversation with someone you trust. Sometimes they hit you like a bolt of lightning. I suggest that you make note on a daily basis of what you are feeling, thinking, believing, and doing. By writing or recording what you are aware of, you will be growing your ability to be conscious of how **Welcoming Change** is removing barriers and blocks to your happy endings in life.

# Key #5 - SALVATION:

## The End of the Suffering

The Universe truly is always working on your behalf. You will know that the Grace of Welcoming Change has been given to you when what you have asked to manifest does so in ways you could never imagine! As I said before, the absence of suffering leaves your mind and emotions with the time and energy to create new experiences, new situations and better relationships. All of that supports and grows your capacity for well-being, kindness, compassion, creativity, joy and love.

# CONGRATULATIONS!

You have used all 5 of your keys to self-mastery and have consciously welcomed change into your life. You have now completed your journey through your inner landscape using the ancient wisdom of the Dagara Medicine Wheel. Know that you may repeat this journey as many times as needed to strengthen and maintain your ability to transform, versus transfer, your emotional pain.

For a virtual acknowledgment for completing your Wisdom Walk healing journey, click on the link below that will take you to my *Wisdom Walk to Self-Mastery* website. Once there, click on "Book Videos" to access the *Nature Ritual and Completion Praise.*

www.wisdomwalktoselfmastery.com

# Presentations Of Learning:
## Documenting Your Healing Experience

Congratulations for completing your **Wisdom Walk to Self-Mastery** healing journey! For the Wisdom Walk to Self-Mastery program, the final class was a graduation ceremony which is called, "**Presentations of Learning**." This is the opportunity for the men to be witnessed by a supportive audience as they share about the healing journey. The idea of Presentations of Learning comes from the Public Allies program, where young leaders serve for ten months at human services agencies in their community. At the end of their tenure, they are asked to respond to the following cloze sentences: I used to be . . .; but now I am . . .

Doing your own personal Presentation of Learning is a wonderful way to begin to consciously integrate all of the new insights and understanding that you have gained from your Wisdom Walk journey. I encourage you to take the time to write about, or record, how the experience of reading this book and using the elemental rituals has helped you to heal and transform your pain and grow beyond who you used to be.

# Part Five
# WISDOM WALKING
# AT THE MOVIES

# INTRODUCTION

$\mathcal{M}$ ovies have always played an important role in my growth, development, and healing. It all began with the technicolor classic, *The Wizard of Oz*. This film was made in Hollywood's golden year of 1939. It was only shown in theaters two more times (1949 and 1955) before being broadcast on American national television. The very first showing was on November 3ʳᵈ, 1956. From 1959 until 1991 it became a much-anticipated annual television event, shown sometime between Thanksgiving and Christmas on a Sunday night.

I began watching *The Wizard of Oz* annually with my sister, Cheryl, and brother, Ralph, at the age of four. When my sister was around age 12, my brother age 11, and me age 9, my mom sat us down and explained what the movie was really about by revealing the symbolism in the film. "Don't you see," she said, being the excellent teacher that she was, "the Scarecrow, the Tin Man, and the Lion are all part of Dorothy's mind. They represent her intellect, her emotions, her fears and courage." Thus began my awareness and never-ending enthusiasm for going deep with movies that have a message.

The five films you will read about in these next five chapters are all stories of personal transformation. The characters will not be the same by the end of their story as when we first met them. All of them are seekers of something more — knowledge, understanding, acceptance, and of course, love. To get to their "more", each has to go through challenges that are emotionally painful. Their journeys through their challenges are what interest us as viewers because we can all relate to the human condition of suffering, healing and growth.

The films I will discuss are: *Antwone Fisher, The Whale Rider, Peaceful Warrior, The Matrix,* and *Groundhog Day.* Through these films you will witness the challenge of forgiving those who neglected and abused you, reconciling the past with the present, pursuing your dreams against all odds, accepting and living your purpose, and the challenge of learning to accept change and reinvent yourself. The main reason I've chosen these films, which I've used in the Wisdom Walk program, is because each in its own way is teaching that you are here to have your happy endings in life. Despite the pain and frustration encountered on their journeys, each main character chooses to stay the course. They each step into vulnerability, let go of their egoic fears, then surrender and trust the process of healing and human evolution. As you will see, whether the film is a deep drama, a sci-fi masterpiece, or a fantastical comedy, you can learn something and be inspired.

It is my great pleasure to share my insights and wisdom about these five movies with you. I know my mom, as my ancestor, was guiding me and cheering me on for continuing the legacy. Warning: there will be spoilers, so if you haven't watched these movies before, you may want to do so before you continue reading. Enjoy this written journey through the inner landscape of cinema!

# Chapter 21

## Forgiveness in Antwone Fisher (2002)

## A little background . . .

*T*his film is based on the best-selling autobiography, *Finding Fish (2001)*, by the real Antwone Fisher. He also wrote the screenplay for the film. This film is perfectly cast. Derek Luke, who was a newcomer at the time, stars in the title role. Denzel Washington, who made his directorial debut with the film, also co-stars as the supportive navy therapist. The film also features the late, great Novella Nelson in the role of child abuser, Mrs. Tate. Novella was a singer and character actress whose long-time career also included Broadway and television. Also worth acknowledging is the brief but powerful performance by Viola Davis as Antwone's mother.

Here's an interesting piece of trivia about the child actor, Malcolm David Kelley, who played Antwone in those harrowing scenes of abuse. Malcolm was ten years old at the time when he played eleven-year old Antwone. In real life, Malcolm spent the first eleven months of his life in foster care before being adopted by a loving family. Since *Antwone Fisher*, he's been consistently working as an actor, including playing a key role as young Walt in the hit TV series "Lost". Most recently he was seen in a powerful role in the 2017 movie *Detroit*. Malcolm also is a singer and rap artist, and he formed a duo called MKTO. He released his first album with his duo partner in 2013.

The producer of this film was inspired to make the film after hearing the story from Mr. Fisher, who at the time was working as a security guard at Sony Pictures movie studios.

Although the film did not receive any Oscar nods, it did win awards from the Black Reel Awards, the Christopher Awards (for producers, directors and writers *who affirm the highest values of the human spirit*), the Humanitas Prize (for screenplays that promote human values), and the American Screenwriters Association. At the 2003 NAACP Annual Awards, Derek Luke was awarded for 'best actor' and 'best breakthrough performance', while Denzel Washington was awarded 'best director'.

## Synopsis of the Film

Antwone Fisher, a young United States Navy recruit, who was born in prison and grew up in foster care, is sent to a naval psychiatrist to learn how to manage his violent outbursts. Failure to do so will mean a dishonorable discharge from the military. After initially resisting the healing opportunity, he finally shares with his therapist his horrendous childhood trauma. With the encouragement of his therapist, and the support of a girlfriend, Antwone goes on a physical, emotional, and spiritual journey to face his demons, and discover the family he never knew he had.

## Why I Chose This Film

Besides the obvious, which is that it's a story of transformation through forgiveness, this film had a deeply personal impact on me. The year this movie was released is the year I experienced my own forgiveness with my estranged father. My mother and father separated just before I was born when it was discovered that he and another woman in the community were also expecting a child together. I didn't grow up with my father, and I never thought I'd need to reconcile anything with him. But, as the Universe would have it, I received a message from a diviner that it would be beneficial for both me and my father for me to make a visit.

Shortly after this divination, I journeyed to where my father was living, first stopping at my aunt's house to get his address. On her kitchen table was a JET magazine, and it featured Denzel Washington's new film, "Antwone Fisher." To make a long story short, I did meet with my father and we did reconcile. He shared his trauma story with me and it changed my life.

About six months later, I was making a usual pit-stop in Cincinnati, at the home of my friend Quanita Roberson, on my way driving from Milwaukee to Washington, DC. After we caught up over roasted chicken at her kitchen table, she placed a copy of a DVD in my hand and told me I had to watch it. In the bedroom, down in the basement where I stayed during my visits, which was beautifully decorated with a Ghanaian mud cloth wall hanging and other precious items related to Africa, I watched *Antwone Fisher*. Several times I had to stop the DVD and just let myself "snot and cry", meaning crying really hard and long. There in 2-D was my father's story. I wasn't just watching a film. I was experiencing one of the most powerful healing events of my life! There's never been a time since my first viewing of this film that I don't shed tears. It will always remain on my list of "The Movies That Changed Your Life."

Another important aspect of this film that I'm so grateful for is it's honoring of the Ancestors. I was blown away when I saw the opening scene. The camera pans, from Antwone's perspective, over two lines of people facing each other dressed in outfits from their particular time period. Right away the film is teaching that the past plays an important role in healing. We're taken on a journey with Antwone Fisher to discover how that plays out. By connecting Antwone to his ancestors right from the start, I believe the film is in alignment with the ancient African wisdom of honoring the ancestors first before taking on a challenge.

# Two Scenes That Teach the Power of Forgiveness

## #1 - Confronting the Abusers

Some of the most emotionally disturbing scenes in this film are of the trauma that Antwone survived as a child in the foster home of Mrs. Tate and her daughter, Nadine. According to noted social scientist and author, Dr. Joy DeGruy, Antwone was a victim of multi-generational trauma which she has termed *post-traumatic slave syndrome (PTSS)*. Basically, Dr. DeGruy teaches that PTSS is a set of maladaptive behaviors, which originated as survival strategies during slavery and its aftermath. These are the ancestral wounds from severe trauma being passed from one generation to another.

These gut-wrenching scenes of physical abuse and implied sexual abuse of children had to be very challenging for both the child and adult actors involved. After watching them, you can't imagine how Antwone could ever do forgiveness of his abusers. Fortunately, his therapist, after hearing his story, educated him about the legacy of slavery within the Black community. He refers him to the book, "The Slave Community," by John W. Blassingame, a foundational text originally published in 1972, about the life and culture of slaves in the antebellum South. He next encourages Antwone to experience the truth about his abuse – that it wasn't his fault.

When we watch Antwone return to the Cleveland neighborhood and the house that was the scene of his twelve years of torment, we just know that a fight is going to break out. Instead, we witness Antwone clearly and calmly do a deep level of forgiveness by expressing his truth. He doesn't want revenge or even an apology from Mrs. Tate and Nadine. He is so clear that the fated meeting is about him freeing himself up from his past. Antwone is able to say and demonstrate through his behavior that he didn't deserve to be treated so horribly. Even when Mrs. Tate goes into denial about her evil behavior, Antwone doesn't lose control of himself. He no longer chooses to be a slave to the pain that was transferred on to him. He was literally able to face his demons without engaging in their insanity.

# #2 - Meeting His Mother for the First Time

This scene is the real climax of the film. We are just as afraid as Antwone is when he's standing outside the door to his mom's apartment. His uncle, who has brought him there, can sense his fear and reassures him that he won't let anything bad happen to him.

When Antwone's mother sees him for the first time since she gave birth to him, she screams and runs into her living room. Antwone follows, sits next to her on the couch, gently places his hand on her shoulder, and lovingly shares the pain of not having her in his life. All his mom does is sit there, barely breathing, with a numbed-out expression on her face. She's clearly in shock and doesn't speak to him or make eye contact. When Antwone kisses her on the cheek, she winces as if he were hurting her. Antwone shares his accomplishments with her, telling her that he is a good man. Once he walks out of the apartment, we see his mom allow her pain-filled tears of shame and guilt roll down her cheeks.

This scene very powerfully and poignantly depicts how forgiveness is letting go of carrying someone else's pain. Antwone doesn't explode into a fit of anger and rage over his mother's inability to connect with him. He can easily see that she is very wounded. He's able to believe that her abandonment of him had nothing to do with him. It wasn't his fault. Forgiving her is not letting her off the hook for what she did. Forgiving her is freeing himself up from the belief that he was disposable.

# Final Thoughts on the Film

*Antwone Fisher* is one of the best films I have ever seen regarding the power of forgiveness to free someone up from their past trauma. It gives the viewer such hope, especially at the end when Antwone's dream of a family feast comes true. He gets to his happy endings in a way he could never have imagined. His ability to understand and practice forgiveness is so inspiring. It changes his life, and it can also change ours.

# Chapter 22

# Peacemaking in The Whale Rider (2002)

## A little background . . .

*L*ike *Antwone Fisher*, this film is also based upon a book by the same name. It was written by Witi Ihimaera, a New Zealand native, who was inspired when looking out at the Hudson River while living in New York City. A whale had come up the Hudson and he could see it spouting out water from its air hole. Mr. Ihimaera began to think of his small coastal village home, Whangara, and the mythology about whales that he learned from his community. Shortly after this whale sighting, he took his young daughters to an action-adventure movie which featured a young boy as the hero. At the end of the film, his daughters asked him why the girls always had to be helpless and rescued by the boys. Within three weeks, Ihimaera wrote a story of a young girl, living in a rural New Zealand community, who gets to be the hero.

That heroine is played in the movie by Keisha Castle-Hughes, who was only 11 years old at the time of filming and had never acted before. Although, she shared in an interview that she had always dreamt of becoming an actress. Keisha was selected out of thousands of Maori (indigenous New Zealanders) school girls. The director considered her a "gift" and believed Keisha would be the heart of the film. She was nominated for an Academy Award as Best Actress, one of the youngest persons to ever be nominated in that category.

## Synopsis of the Film

What do you do when you're a Maori chief of a small, impoverished indigenous village on the coast of southern New Zealand, with the responsibility of insuring that the line of chiefs is not broken, when your only grandson dies at birth leaving his twin sister as your only heir? To make matters even more complex, after the death of his wife and son, your eldest son decides to move to Germany to pursue a career as an artist. This is the great challenge faced by Koro, a proud elder committed to maintaining his culture and spiritual traditions in the aftermath of colonialism, and the onslaught of modernity.

Much to Koro's chagrin, his surviving granddaughter, Pikea, who was defiantly named after the ancient founding father of their community by her father, consistently demonstrates the traditional leadership qualities of a true heir to the throne. Koro's tradition forbids a woman becoming the chief, but Pikea's courage and unconditional love for her grandfather are about to change all that.

## Why I Chose This Movie

Working with an all-male group in the *Wisdom Walk to Self-Mastery* program, I thought it was important for the men to see a story about how a man's belief in females as disposable is transformed to believe that they are Divine. *Whale Rider* is a brilliant and rare female initiation story. Pikea goes through a heroine's journey, where her biggest dragon to slay is the grandfather she adores. As a result, the viewer is also treated to the grandfather's journey through guilt, shame and blame which in the end brings him to reconciliation and peace.

# Scenes Deserving of Attention

Honestly, there are no wasted scenes in *Whale Rider*. Every scene in this movie is a gem of movie-making. We are emotionally pulled into the story from the opening scene of Pikea's mom in gut-wrenching labor. We witness the love of family and community through Koro riding Pikea on the handle bars of his bike, and Nanny Flowers, Pikea's grandma, performing the chants for the opening ceremony of the leadership school. Then, there is Pikea's tearful delivery of her speech honoring Koro, and of course, Pikea riding the Whale in her willingness to die. For the purpose of showing how the movie teaches about peacemaking, I will focus on Koro's story. It is all about the barriers to peacemaking.

Through Koro's story, we better understand how guilt and shame result in blame, even of people we may dearly love. When we are first introduced to him, we can clearly see that Koro is burdened by his role as chief of Whangara. This is greatly due to the post-colonial poverty and the pressures of honoring and maintaining ancient traditions in the modern world. The death of his only grandson leaves Koro angry and ashamed. It is his responsibility to maintain the line of chiefs. Instead of accepting his granddaughter, Pikea, as the way forward to make that happen, Koro blames her for his downfall.

Watch carefully the scenes in which Koro is discouraging her, accusing her, and ignoring the true leader that she is. These scenes really illustrate how we can be so attached to what we know that we become unable to consider learning something new. It's not until Koro is at Pikea's bedside in the hospital, knowing now that it was her spirit and wisdom that saved the whales, that finally he is willing and able to reconcile the past with the present.

# Final Thoughts on the Film

My favorite scene in this movie is the joyous and uplifting happy ending. Seeing Koro sitting beside Pikea in the Dragon boat always brings tears to my eyes. You can see that he is fully accepting of her, and at peace with his role as her mentor and guide. Within this scene is also an affirmation of how the members of the community have reclaimed their ancient traditions. Their daily poverty is no longer an impediment to their feeling proud and valuing themselves. In a voice over, we hear Pikea affirming her belief that leadership is to be shared. The closing scene seems to say, "Everyone must be a leader in their own domain so that loving community can exist." This peaceful, happy ending we get to witness is rooted in the belief that there are no disposable people. This is a message all human beings need to receive on a daily basis.

# Chapter 23

# Valuing Self in Peaceful Warrior (2006)

## A little background . . .

*T*his film is based on the 1980 best seller, *Way of the Peaceful Warrior*, written by Dan Millman as a quasi-autobiography. He mixes his real-life experiences as a gymnast, with some spiritual fiction to create what he calls, "a book that will change lives." The core of the story is based on Dan's traumatizing motorcycle accident in 1966, which happened just before his senior year at the University of California-Berkeley. He shattered his right femur and had to have a bone marrow transplant and a steel nail inserted in his femur. As a result of his difficult and successful rehabilitation, he was able to return to gymnastics as co-captain of his team. They won the 1968 NCAA Gymnastics Championships. At the competition, Dan was the last man to perform. His performance on the high bar was a best-ever routine and his perfect landing clinched the team title. That same year, he was voted *Senior U.C. Berkeley Athlete of the Year* and graduated with a B.A. degree in Psychology.

Dan credits the inspiration for his first book to a gas station attendant he met who reminded him of the Greek philosopher, Socrates. From the Amazon.com editorial review of the film, Dan is quoted as saying,

> *I did meet an old service station mechanic about three a.m. on a starry morning. And I did call him "Socrates." He impacted my life not only with his*

*words, but with the light in his eyes and the way he carried himself — and he became the archetypal Mentor described in my book.*

## Synopsis of the Film

The lead character in this film, Dan Millman, is a gifted gymnast and Olympic hopeful attending the UC at Berkeley. He is also self-absorbed, arrogant, egotistical, and suffering from anxiety. As the film opens, we view Dan's nightmare about falling and shattering his leg. This dream foreshadows Dan's motorcycle accident. The dream also contains a glimpse of someone's shoes as they sweep up the shattered glass-like pieces of his leg. Unable to sleep after the nightmare, Dan makes a 3am snack food run to a gas station, where he meets Socrates and notices that he's wearing the same shoes from his dream.

When Dan turns to leave then looks back, Socrates has miraculously gotten up on the roof of the gas station. Awed by this gravity defying feat, Dan asks Socrates to be his teacher. Socrates agrees, but the restrictions and practices required are not what Dan expected. When things literally fall apart for Dan, it's Socrates who guides and supports him through an emotional, spiritual, and physical healing journey.

## Why I Chose This Film

*Peaceful Warrior* does an excellent job of sharing wisdom for self-mastery, while depicting realistically the process of having to let go of who you thought you were in order to become who you are truly. I usually showed this movie after the men in the Wisdom Walk program had settled into the program's healing practices and discipline. The film provided an effective way for the men to be validated in their own journey towards self-mastery. It also contains some memorable scenes and words of wisdom that can be easily recalled, and this served as inspiration and hope for the men.

I also appreciate how *Peaceful Warrior* shows that healing is something we choose to do, or not. No one can really heal us but ourselves. The film depicts Socrates, played masterfully by actor Nick Nolte, as the ultimate mentor and guide. Although Socrates is very wise he is also humble. He never tries to control Dan or feel sorry for him. He is able to solidly and lovingly hold space for Dan as Dan takes on the responsibility of learning to truly love and value himself.

# My Favorite Scenes and Wisdom Phrases

## #1 - Socrates Throws Dan Off of the Bridge:

Based on the Dagara Medicine Wheel teachings, this is a scene of a radical water ritual. At this point in his journey, Dan really needed it, as we all do when we have forgotten to slow down and pay attention to what is happening right in front of us. You can't access your truth or connect to your soul by staying busy and rushing around all the time. It is easy to allow people, places and things that have no direct bearing on the achievement of our goals distract us to no end. Staying consciously awake to ourselves and the world around us requires attention and focus. Becoming present is a choice, and a hard one to make in this modern world of endless schedules and instant messages.

Dan's reaction to being unexpectedly thrown off the bridge by his mentor is to feel victimized. Isn't that the same way we feel when there's a power outage and all of our technology and gadgets stop working? It's only when Socrates takes him by the shoulders and enables him to really see that, "**there's never nothing going on**," that Dan realizes how much he's missing by always rushing around. Unfortunately, he doesn't put this learning into practice and later in the film he ends up running a red light.

This bridge sequence ends with Socrates telling him, "**Take out the trash, Dan!**" He's referring to how Dan is holding onto the past and having anxiety about the future, both of which we have no control over. Socrates then whispers into Dan's wet ear before walking away, "**When you are in the here and now, you will be amazed at what you can do, and how well you can do it!**"

## #2 - Confronting the Shadow/Pain Body

Besides the Gollum versus Sméagol scene in the second part of the *Lord of the Rings Movie Trilogy*, Dan confronting his 'shadow self' is one of the best I've ever seen. This scene occurs right after Dan is told by his coach that he's been denied acceptance into the Olympic trials. This bad news throws Dan into the lowest point of his life. All his long, hard work with gymnastics, endless hours of rehabilitation, and even the higher consciousness training with Socrates did not help, or so he thinks. We watch him take out his rage on all his awards and medals before going up to the clock tower to end it all.

His face to face with his pain body on the ledge of the clock tower is done brilliantly. It's so easy to relate to this scene because we all have that negative voice in our heads that tries really hard to run our lives. Seeing the pain body embodied as your twin, who wants you to believe they're the one keeping you going, is both unnerving and true. Notice that Dan is able to let go of his evil twin even though he says he doesn't know what he's doing or what the consequences will be. This is what I call faith! There is a YouTube clip of this scene titled, "Letting

Go of the Ego." I watch it when I want to be reminded that my pain body does not have to control me.

# #3 - The Hike Up the Mountain

I really appreciate this scene for how it teaches not only about the journey being more fulfilling than the arrival at the destination, but about how learning is continuous. The scene opens just before Dan and Socrates reach the top of the mountain they've been climbing for over three hours. Socrates has spent the time quizzing Dan on some of the teachings about being a peaceful warrior. Dan demonstrates his knowledge of paradox (*Life is a mystery; don't waste time trying to figure it out*), humor (*keep a sense of humor, especially about yourself*), and change (*no one and nothing ever stays the same*). Then we witness Dan lose it when Socrates tells him that he came all that way just to see a rock, that even Socrates himself didn't know would be there.

In response to Dan's complaining, Socrates reminds him of how happy he was during their journey to the top. He helps him realize how he allowed his disappointment and judgement of what was waiting squash his enthusiasm and excitement. This is a powerful lesson about the wisdom of avoiding attachment to external, temporal things, and to stay focused on what really matters: being present and enjoying those moments. This scene also brilliantly messages how despite our accumulation of higher knowledge and wisdom, there is always more to learn. Our journey to self-mastery is never-ending.

# #4 - The Closing Scene

In the final scene of *Peaceful Warrior*, Dan has come full circle in his healing journey. Just as in indigenous initiations for children to become adults, Dan returns to where he started -- but now his is different. He is no longer that arrogant, egotistical, and scared young man we met at the opening of the movie. As he's holding onto the still rings to begin his routine in the competition, we hear the voiceover of Socrates ask him these three centering questions:

| | |
|---|---|
| Socrates: | *Where are you?* |
| Dan: | *Here!* |
| Socrates: | *What time is it?* |
| Dan: | *Now!* |
| Socrates: | *Who are you?* |
| Dan: | *This moment!* |

This sums up the true meaning of valuing self. You are able to be in the present and open to learning what the moment holds for you. You are not comparing yourself to others. You trust that you will do the best that you can do, and that this is the true measure of your worth. To value oneself means to accept and love yourself unconditionally.

## Final Thoughts on the Film

When asked what his thoughts were on the final cut of the film, Dan Millman said, "*Peaceful Warrior* reflects a new genre — "cinema with substance" — transformational film." (*Amazon.com editorial review – interview with Dan Millman*)
I wholeheartedly agree with him.

# Chapter 24

# Remembering Purpose in
# The Matrix (1999)

## A little background . . .

The first film in *The Matrix Trilogy* came at the end of the 20th century. It was released into theatres in March of 1999, and by December of that year it was released on both VHS (video) and DVD formats. It became the first DVD to sell more than one million copies in the US. The film is typically regarded as one of the greatest science fiction films of all time, and in 2012 it was selected for preservation in the National Film Registry of the Library of Congress as "culturally, historically, and aesthetically significant."

The film is also shrouded in controversy. A Black woman named, Sophia Stewart, attempted to sue the Wachowski's, the sibling team who are credited with writing the screenplay and directing the film. She accused them of stealing her ideas, which she sent to them in response to their 1986 solicitation of sci-fi stories to be made into comic books. She claims she never heard back from them, and when she first saw the film, she recognized her story, "The Third Eye." Although urban legend says she won her law suit, there is no information on the web to confirm that. She does have a website where she pronounces herself as "The Mother of the Matrix."

*The Matrix* film is also associated with the horrific Columbine High School shootings. Although it's special effects were ground-breaking and won several awards, including an Oscar, the film's graphic depiction of gun violence set to alternative rock music had a deadly influence on the impressionable minds of the teen shooters. They were dressed similar to the main character when he storms a high-rise office building to rescue his mentor.

Despite its heartbreaking controversies, the mythology and messages in *The Matrix* are potent, mind-bending, and relevant. It is truly an important film for the beginning of the 21$^{st}$ century. It asks us to question how we might be enslaved to a survival-driven, technologically advanced culture that doesn't know how to recognize or support our sacred human need for meaning and purpose in life.

## Synopsis of the Film

In a time unknown in the future, the highly anticipated and heralded creation of artificial intelligence (AI) has resulted in machines taking over the world. The machines have created a virtual reality for humans, who they can breed and use as their energy source. The main character, Thomas Anderson, also known as Neo, is a typical 9-5 young urban professional during the day, and a notorious computer hacker by night. As the story begins, we learn that he is obsessed with finding a man named Morpheus, who he believes has information about "The Matrix," a mystery on the web which Neo feels driven to solve. When Neo is unexpectedly contacted by Morpheus's associate, Trinity, for a meeting, his life will never be the same. Not only does he learn what the Matrix is, but he is told, and to his chagrin, that he is considered a saviour. Neo is resistant to being "The One" who can end the war and save the human world, until he is faced with the choice to save Morpheus or himself.

# Why I Chose This Film

I was introduced to *The Matrix* in at the beginning of the year 2000 by my friend and mentor, Queen Noor Jawad. We were both committed to higher consciousness learning and were continuously reading and discussing works by Deepak Chopra, Ken Wilber, Jon Kabat Zen, Pema Chodron, Caroline Myss, and other authors of New Age spirituality, and human potential. We viewed *The Matrix* several times, each time diving deeper into the mythological, philosophical, and spiritual references we understood. We appreciated how intelligently and creatively some of what we knew as very esoteric information was being presented. Our excitement for the New Age script, and the surprising casting of Black actors in significant roles, had us disregard the film's graphic gun violence. The film gave us new vocabulary for people and events that were operating out of old belief systems and paradigms – *they were locked in the Matrix.*

One year later, I had the opportunity to watch *The Matrix* frequently, at least once a week, over a five-month period. It was released to HBO cable television, and I had returned to my family home to help care for my mother. She was terminally ill with lung cancer. Like Neo, I was in a deep emotional, physical, and spiritual transition as my world was being turned completely upside down. *The Matrix* movie became my 'cinematic medicine.' It helped me focus on the importance of knowing and enacting my true purpose. I couldn't imagine who I could be without my mother to blame, to challenge, and to love. Every time I viewed it, the movie revealed more questions for me to contemplate about who I truly was, why was I born, and how and why was I not living on purpose. When my mother died on June 21, 2001, the first day of summer, I was clear that I had to go out and meet my purpose. I was ready to go on my own journey of healing, growth and evolution. *The*

*Matrix* film helped to launch me on my quest. (Those details are for another book!)

## Three Powerful Scenes About Remembering Purpose

Dear Reader, you really need to know that I could write (and perhaps I will) an entire book about all the scenes in *The Matrix*, giving my analysis of their mythological and spiritual meaning. For this book, though, I will share three of the scenes I think most powerfully support the remembering of purpose.

## #1 - Blue Pill or Red Pill:

One of the most important and iconic scenes in this film is Neo's highly anticipated initial meeting with Morpheus, who's played superbly by actor Lawrence Fishburne. It is during this meeting that Morpheus gives Neo a choice between the red pill or the blue pill. Taking the red pill will enable Neo to experience his long sought-after answer to, "what is the Matrix?" Taking the blue pill will erase his memory and return him to life as he has known it.

I believe this scene wonderfully symbolizes the choice that everyone has to make on the quest to live on purpose. If you are not aware of your true purpose and living it, then you are just surviving and going along with someone else's program. Like Neo at the beginning of *The Matrix*, you will live a life of quiet desperation. By this, I mean that something inside of you wants to be let loose, but you're too afraid to let that happen.

Neo being confronted with the choice between the red and blue pills is symbolic of the opportunities that emerge in our lives to help us move forward to having a purposeful life. For example, anyone who is diagnosed with a life-threatening illness, or who unexpectedly loses their job, or who is facing a prison sentence, has the opportunity to choose to radically change their lives or continue on with business as usual. The red pill symbolizes the willingness to go on a journey of waking up to true purpose. The blue pill is the symbol of saying 'NO' to healing, growth, and evolution.

Neo chooses the red pill, and this begins his serious transformation. After almost dying in the Matrix when Morpheus and his team are working to free him, we see Neo wake up to his three-dimensional environment. It is a body capsule full of red gelatinous material, and he's plugged into tubes that feed him and control his virtual reality. His waking up gets him flushed down a giant tube to be disposed of in the sewer, but he's rescued by Morpheus and his crew on the airship, Nebuchadnezzar. Neo is welcomed to the "real world" and his naked, hairless body is like that of a new born. This is symbolic to how very vulnerable you feel when stepping onto the path of remembering purpose. You know what you've left behind, but you don't know what you've come into. The *blue pill or red pill'* scene does a great job illustrating that stepping onto the path of remembering purpose is challenging, but it is a choice. Once you've made the choice to take the red pill and wake up to the truth of who you are, you will never go back to sleep.

## #2 - The Visit to The Oracle

This is a scene I really appreciate, and not only because of the amazing actress who plays the Oracle, Ms. Gloria Foster. This scene is about our resistance to living on purpose. I connect Neo's visit to the Oracle to getting still and connecting to your higher self. The Oracle symbolizes the higher knowing that we all possess inside of us. As I discussed previously in Chapter 9, everyone is born full of purpose and it is the responsibility of parents and community to help us remember what we already know. But, without this developmental support, like Neo at the onset of the film, we will be seeking our purpose without even knowing it.

When Neo meets the Oracle, she detects his disbelief in himself. She tells him he has the "gift" but he's not using it, so he's not "The One." Neo seems relieved to hear this, and this is true for most of us. I believe the reason for the hesitancy to claim and embrace true purpose is that many things in your life will change, and you will be transformed. There will be certain people, places, and possessions from which you'll need to detach and let go. This is a painful process. Your life focus moves away from just being about you and your survival needs to being about how you serve others. In serving others, you will receive everything you need to be happy and healthy, but none of us enjoys outgrowing who we once were.

As I shared in the second chapter of this book, my most favorite line from *The Matrix* comes as Neo is being driven to see the Oracle. It is his first time experiencing what he now knows is a computer-generated virtual reality. He's sitting in the back seat of the black Lincoln sedan next to Trinity, and he's looking out of the window at places in his neighborhood where he used to eat and shop. He's still very much in awe about the existence of the Matrix and asks Trinity, *"What does it all mean?"* Her right-on response is, *"That the Matrix cannot tell you who you are!"* Wow! The same is true about anything external and temporal within your own existence. The truth of who you are is not how much money you have in your bank account, how luxurious your home, or how white your teeth! The truth of who you are lies solely in your higher purpose. When all of the external and material things change or disappear from your life, the who you are truly will still exist.

Resisting our purpose in life may be a natural human reaction, but it's not something we want to do for the rest of our lives. We are all "The One" in our unique ability to make our contributions to the health and well-being of others. Even though there is stuff that has to be left behind, it will be replaced by the joy of knowing that you matter, that you are valuable and valued, loving and loved, and not disposable but Divine.

# #3 - Stopping Bullets

As stated at the beginning of this section, I could write a whole book on *The Matrix* and it's spiritual and higher consciousness messages. The final scene I'll share with you is what I consider to be the climax of the film. At this point in the story, we know that if a human is plugged into the Matrix, and is killed in that virtual reality, they will also die in the real world. We also know that Mr. Smith and his team of Agents are unstoppable. They can't be killed because they are not human. They're artificial intelligence (AI). So, when any human encounters them, the rule is to run away as fast as you can. Now, Agent Smith is Neo's nemesis/villain and represents the pain body. As Neo becomes more willing to access and use his unique powers and gifts, Agent Smith becomes even more of a threat to him. In a final battle, Smith kills Neo in the Matrix.

In a twist, the film does a huge gender-reversed nod to the fairytale *Sleeping Beauty* as Trinity revives Neo in the real world with a kiss. Smith and his look-alike Agents are shocked to see Neo come back to life and fire off a hail of bullets to kill him again. This time, Neo puts out his hand and stops the bullets in mid-air. He's fully able to believe that the Matrix is just an illusion, and he chooses not to be its victim anymore. He remembers his purpose.

Just as Neo does in this scene, we can also reach our turning point, reclaim our power over our pain body, and emerge as "The One" who frees us up from our past story of pain.

Remembering purpose is the key. It enables you to believe that you always have a choice as to whether or not you allow your pain body to rule and run your life. Saying "No" to the pain body is like stopping bullets.

## Final Thoughts on the Film

According to the website, www.Ranker.com, the number one quote out of all three Matrix movies, ranked by fans, comes from the first film and was spoken by Morpheus to Neo: "*This is your last chance. After this, there is no turning back. You take the blue pill - the story ends, you wake up in your bed and believe whatever you want to believe. You take the red pill - you stay in Wonderland and I show you how deep the rabbit-hole goes.*" Enough said.

# Chapter 25

## Welcoming Change in
## Groundhog Day (1993)

### A little background . . .

$G$ roundhog Day was released onto the screen back in 1993. It was one of those low-budget, G-rated comedies that the producers hoped would turn enough profit to cover the production costs. It stars Bill Murray, one of the few *Saturday Night Live* alumni to cross over into a successful film career. The film is directed by his friend, and the co-star of the original *Ghostbusters*, Harold Ramis. The movie did well at the box office and received decent reviews, but nobody would have believed that thirteen years later it would be selected to be preserved in the United States Library of Congress among great movies like *Citizen Kane* or *Lawrence of Arabia*.

The screenplay for *Groundhog Day* is ranked #27 on the list of the *101 Greatest Screenplays*, according to the Writers Guild of America. In 2008, the American Film Institute (AFI) named this film #8 on the list of the *Top Ten Fantasy Films of Hollywood*. This film is definitely a classic and has had a lasting impact. The phrase "Groundhog Day" has become slang for an unpleasant situation that continually repeats. The town where the movie was filmed, Woodstock, Illinois, has been holding an annual Groundhog Day Festival since 1993, complete with screenings of the movie and a walking tour of the locations used for the film. Also, on February 2nd, 2016, in Liverpool, England, fans participated in a marathon showing of the film, watching it twelve times in a row, over a 24-hour period. I'm sure most of the fans who participated at the 56-seat Smalls Cinema, were younger than 40 years old. It was an opportunity to experience a bit of what the story was about. Clearly, the legacy of this film continues with a whole new generation of moviegoers.

## Synopsis of the Film

*Groundhog Day* is the story of Phil Connors, a middle-aged, run-of-the-mill television weatherman. When we first meet him he is not happy with himself or anyone around him. He's arrogant, sarcastic, and stuck in a mediocre job. When he's sent on assignment to cover the annual Groundhog Day event in Punxsutawney, Pennsylvania, his life will never be the same. An unexpected snow storm causes him and his news team to stay overnight in Punxsutawney. When he wakes up the next morning, he discovers that he is reliving the day before. Thus begins Phil's transformational journey, with lots of comedy, to becoming more than he ever thought was possible.

## Why I Chose This Film

I first began watching *Groundhog Day* on an annual basis back in 2002. It was one of several films that I relied upon to keep me inspired and focused during my six and a half-years as a nomad, learning to embrace my gift as a shamanic healer. The film's story raised my consciousness about how we can negatively judge and resist the situations that God and the Universe have designed uniquely for our growth and development.

*Groundhog Day* really helped me learn the importance of surrendering to the greater will of a Greater Order and Direction as I was opening myself up to learning how to change the only thing in my life over which I had any control -- my Self. So, instead of whining and complaining when a new or different situation showed up on my journey, I chose to patiently wait and be shown what healing and growth opportunities there were in it for me. I did put up some resistance at first, because I'm human, but that didn't last very long.

I also chose this film to illustrate the importance of welcoming change because it does it so cleverly and with humor. I just love the way the script and the actors use humor so appropriately to open the viewer to the deeply philosophical and spiritual question: *what would you do if you had to live the same day over and over again?* I believe the most inspirational theme in this movie is the power of choice. This is something so essential to healing and growth. We have to choose it to experience it and receive the rewards.

## My Favorite Scenes on Phil's Journey to Welcoming and Embracing Change

### #1 - The Adolescent Behavior Response

Early in my career, I had the benefit of knowing an expert in adolescent development, Dr. Peter Scales, who taught me that there are four questions every teenager needs to hear "Yes" to on a daily basis, but usually doesn't: (1) Am I normal? (2) Am I capable? (3) Do I belong? (4) Am I loved and loving? These are also the questions that are driving Phil Connors as he steps into his Groundhog Day experience. At first, he reacts to endlessly living through the same day just like a typical developing teenager. He decides he's Superman and can do anything he wants without any consequences.

The first scene of this adolescent behavior occurs when he hooks up with Ralph and Gus, two drunk locals at the bowling alley, who he takes on a wild ride speeding through town, destroying a mailbox, getting chased by the police, riding along railroad tracks and daring an oncoming train, and then declaring that he's not going to abide by anyone's rules anymore. This scene so captures the way in which most humans react to change – we resist. We will look for ways and means to do everything else but open up to the challenging and often painful experience of change. Like Phil Connors, we'll attempt to make up what we think the change is all about, rather than opening up to learning what it's really all about. The problem with this is that there are consequences to resisting change. For Phil, it is boredom that turns into despair. He can't escape from his Groundhog Day, no matter how many times he smashes the alarm clock or kills himself. He doesn't yet know that he has the ability to choose to experience his time loop from a totally different perspective.

## #2 - The Control Drama Reaction

When Phil realizes that being naughty gets boring and that he can't change the day in which he's stuck, he decides to take on a courtship of Rita, his producer and the woman to whom he's really attracted. Unfortunately, at this point in his journey, Phil Connors has no idea what is truly love because he doesn't love himself. He attaches himself to the idea that he can make Rita fall in love and have sex with him. You know this isn't going to end well.

During his controlling courtship, we witness Phil's failed attempts to manipulate Rita. He uses his time looping to find out everything he can about her life, her likes and her dislikes. He plans out his time and conversation with her to portray himself as what she has shared is her ideal man. To his great dismay, he discovers that neither time, money, or information can get Rita to do what he wants her to do. Rita is always able to see right through Phil's game, and she repeatedly rejects his attempts to make love to her with a hard slap to his face.

This compilation of Phil's manipulative courtship scenes

clearly illustrates how when change threatens our ability to know what's coming, we may look for someone or something to fill our need for control. Just like being a rule-breaking Superman, Phil again realizes that control dramas also have consequences. Realizing that he can't have the woman he wants, or a forward-moving life, Phil decides the only thing left is to kill himself. But, even that doesn't work.

## #3 - The "I'm a God" Scene

After several failed attempts to kill himself, Phil finally opens himself up to learning. Although he initially sought help from Rita, a medical doctor, and a highly inexperienced therapist when his time loop first began, he wasn't in a place of acceptance. This time in a conversation with Rita to share what's happening to him, he is totally accepting that Groundhog Day is his reality. Although he starts his conversation with what sounds arrogant, "I'm a God," we witness him expressing vulnerability and honesty. At this point in his journey, Phil Connors has finally gotten flat, meaning he's let go of his resistance. Notice that the scene right before this conversation with Rita is of him jumping off the roof of the courthouse.

Having nothing else to do to control his situation, Phil lets go of trying to make up what is happening to him, or why it's happening to him. He surrenders to the fact that he doesn't know and opens himself up to learning. It is his choosing to risk not being taken seriously by Rita that has her respond with genuine compassion and kindness. Her kind words of wisdom, *"Hey Phil, maybe this isn't so bad,"* sparks a shift in his consciousness and attitude toward his situation. She spends the day and night with him to bear witness to the time loop. He realizes that he really loves her, and he does want to transform himself into her ideal man. He wakes up the next morning not with anger, confusion or fear, but with a willingness to make something good and meaningful out of his time loop. As viewers, we are happy to see him finally step fully into welcoming and eventually embracing change.

## #4 - The Death of the Old Man and Phil's Transformation

The scene that most affects me in *Groundhog Day* is the death of the old man. It is in this scene that Phil Connors learns that having free will and choice does not mean you have control over everything.

When Phil finally wakes up to the possibility of his time loop as the opportunity to change himself, one of the first things he chooses to do is help the old man who is begging on the corner he passes in the morning. At first Phil gives him all the money he has in his pocket, but when he discovers the old man unconscious in an alley one night, he decides to try and save him. He befriends the old man by treating him to a good meal in the coffee shop. Despite Phil's efforts and generosity, the old man still continues to die in the alley each night.

Phil initially refuses to believe that the old man had to die. It's inferred through the scenes that he makes several attempts to keep death from doing its job. Finally, when the old man is dying in his arms once again, Phil raises his head and eyes up to the heavens. In this poignant, emotion-laden moment, we witness Phil finally accepting God's Will. It was just the old man's time to die.

Like Phil Connors, we all come to learn the difference between choice and control. When a change situation shows up in our lives, we do get to choose how we want to react and respond. We do not get to choose the details of what we experience or the duration of our experience. That is a level of control reserved for a Greater Order and Direction. That is the mystery of our journey to our happy endings in life.

After he accepts that he cannot stop someone from dying when it is their time, Phil chooses to put his time and energy into growing himself. He learns how to play the piano and ice sculpt. He becomes a chiropractic. He also keeps a daily schedule of service to people in need in his adopted small-town community. Every day he performs the Heimlich maneuver on a man choking in a restaurant and catches a boy who always falls from a tree. Phil's commitment to learning and service, which is very much in alignment with Buddhist philosophy, is what eventually releases him from his time loop. He and Rita come together and agree to marry and live in Punxsutawney.

## Final Thoughts on the Film

The big question for most people who view this film is, "How many years was Phil Connors stuck in Groundhog Day?" On the web, director Harold Ramis is quoted as saying Phil was trapped for 10 years, even though the original plan was to have him trapped for 10,000 years. Fans of the movie also have their "guesstimates". One website called *Wolf Gnards* ran the numbers and determined that it was eight years, eight months and sixteen days. Yet in 2014, the website *WhatCulture* combined various time duration assumptions and estimated that Phil spent a total of 12,395 days—just under **34 years**— reliving Groundhog Day.

Despite how long his time loop was, the important piece in the story is what he finally decided to do with his time. The same can be true for all of us who choose to welcome change. We can shift from being a victim to circumstance and step into a life of purpose, meaning and never-ending happy endings.

# Closing Prayer

Dear Reader:

*J*t has been my great pleasure to share the Wisdom Walk to Self-Mastery and the ancient wisdom of the Dagara Medicine Wheel with you. It is my great desire that you have received at least one word of wisdom or one insight that supports you in either becoming or staying the best version of your Self. Thank you for taking this journey with me. May you always choose to transform your pain and live your happy endings to their fullest.

*Dear Creator, Mother-Father, God, Source, All The One, All That Is,*
*Thank you for blessing me with the remembrance of my higher purpose.*
*Thank you for enabling me to be a vessel for your divine energy.*
*Thank you for enabling me to receive the blessing of words meant for healing.*
*Thank you for providing me with everything I needed to bring this book into this dimension*
*and into the hands of this reader.*
*May your loving presence continue to flow and imbue each reader with an open mind,*
*and open heart,*
*and an open will*
*to walk their wisdom, share their love and live a life of fulfillment and endless happy endings.*
*Ashé!*

# Acknowledgments

*T*he writing of this book was a 10-year process for me. During this decade, I have been stretched and grown beyond belief and travelled across the United States. I created my outline for the book in Milwaukee, Wisconsin in December of 2008, but it wasn't until January of 2015 in Phoenix, Arizona that I got my right writing voice. Then from July to August of that year, the first five chapters flowed onto my yellow notepads at Ms. Ali's home in Sun City West, Arizona, continued in the fall of that year in Ms. Carolyn's home, also in Sun City West, and completion came in 2018 at Ms. Sara's home and Café Zella in Santa Monica, California. I could not have written this book without the physical, financial, emotional, and spiritual support and encouragement of the loving, kind and generous people whose names I will share below.

Cheryl and Michael Boyd, Denise and John Sullivan, Quanita Roberson, Gail Phoenix, aka Queen Angelina Black Raven Heartsong, Carmen Ray, Tamra Stark, Alison Kaminsky, Carolyn Sodini, Mona and Don Williams, Joyce Pokorny, Carmen Pitre, and Sara Sherman Drapkin, thank you for opening your homes to me when I had to leave mine, and for sharing food, a bed or a couch, transportation, financial and other resources so I had no excuse not to write. And, thank you so much for your loving encouragement to finish the book!

Dr. Robert Fox of Shalem Healing Arts in Milwaukee, thank you so much for practicing the Hippocratic oath and being wise enough to know how to help me get physically strong to complete this book. I am forever in your debt and am so grateful to be among those fortunate enough to receive your gift of healing and humanism.

Lyn Magnarini, thank you for your enthusiasm and

encouragement about writing a book; you really helped me believe I could finally make it happen!

Shelby Keefe, I can't thank you enough for offering to design my cover and to apply your artistic genius, and amazing skill as an impressionist, to imaging the Dagara Medicine Wheel. You said you wanted to make sure my cover was top notch, and you certainly have.

Jeveaux Gall, Senior Publishing Agent at Balboa Press, thank you for believing in my book outline and keeping my dream of being published alive through continuous emailing and phone calling for 4 years! And thank you to all of the staff at Balboa Press and Hay House for being there for authors who see beyond the three-dimensional reality.

Nina, Marina, Karina, Vivian, Alan and all staff of Café Zella in Santa Monica, thank you for maintaining such a welcoming, warm, delicious, nurturing neighborhood eatery that has become my second home.

Nancy Petoskey, thank you for storing all my stuff in your basement and closets all these years, for putting in so much time during your summer vacation to help me edit the book, for sharing your children (Kyle, Ian, and Isabella) with me, and for always reminding me of the truth of who I am when my pain body tries to convince me of something else.

Terri Strodthoff, James Mosely, Bennie Higgins, Kitonga Alexander, Stephen Christopher, and Floyd Rowell, II, thank you for being the bedrock of the Alma Center and supporting the Wisdom Walk to Self-Mastery and the culture it spawned for professional development. Thank you for your trust and love and help with validating my ideas and methodology for integrating spirituality into human services. And a big thank you to all of the Alma Center staff past, present, and future for your commitment to helping men reinvent their lives so their children can be free.

I am so grateful for my entire family, but especially my sister Cheryl and my brother Ralph. Thank you for loving me unconditionally, for praying for me, and for being the only other people on the planet who know what it was like to eat cocktail franks and watch "The Flintstones" with Dolores.

Thank you to all those I haven't named but who in some way, shape, or form have contributed to my ability to write and publish this book.

And, last but not least, I want to thank Malidoma Somé, the late Sobonfu Somé, and the Elders and community members of the village of Dano in Burkina Faso, West Africa, for sharing the Dagara Medicine Wheel and its ancient wisdom with the world. Barka! Thank you for helping me remember my medicine. Barka! Thank you for reconnecting me with my African ancestors. Barka! May this book honor all of our existence. Ashé!

# An Opportunity to Give
# Back to Indigenous Elders
# of The Dagara Tribe

The ancient wisdom I share in this book would be lost to the world were it not for the brave Elders of the Dagara Tribe. For centuries, colonialism in Africa demonized and outlawed the use of indigenous spiritual traditions. Fortunately, the Dagara Elders of those times found ways to insure that enough of their ancient spiritual beliefs would survive. Through the legacy of their wisdom and insight, Malidoma and Sobonfu Somé were recruited to travel to Europe and America to share the Dagara Medicine Wheel, as well as elemental rituals and community wisdom. I am among many people of all races and nationalities who have now greatly benefitted from the commitment of the Dagara Elders to keep this ancient wisdom alive and walking proudly upon the Earth in modern times. And, having read this book and experienced healing, you are too!

**AVIELA, Inc.,** meaning in Dagara, *"It is all good and well intentioned"*, is a 501 (c) (3) that has been created to offer us the opportunity to express our gratitude to the elders and diviners, the healers and shamans of West Africa, who have been so generous with their time, knowledge, and dedication to the ancestors in continuous support for Elder Malidoma's work in the west. They have dedicated their time and energy, often, without any compensation or acknowledgement. The work they do for us, in the modern world often requires that they take time from doing the work to keep their families fed.

**AVIELA** provides a container for saying "thank you", in a monetary way. I invite you to join me in giving back and helping to support African indigenous wisdom at its source. All contributions, small and large, make a difference in Africa.

**AVIELA** also provides a vehicle to move Elder Malidoma closer to his vision of having a training/healing/retreat center, a home for the Ancestors, here in the west. This place is dedicated to the ongoing offering of ritual training, teaching and intense experiential healing. It will, indeed, become a representation of "the village being reborn in the heart of the modern world". Your gift to **AVIELA**, combined with your vision of healing intention, can become the alchemical medicine that perpetuates healing for individuals, communities, societies, and the world.

**To make a donation through PayPal**, please go online to the following address: http://malidoma.com/main/aviela/

**By Check or Money Order:** make payable to "AVIELA, Inc",

**Mail your donation to the treasurer of AVIELA, Inc.:**

Robert D. Walker
PO Box 82
Cherry Plain, NY 12040
Email: robertdwalker250@gmail.com

*Thank you for considering to give reciprocity in this manner.*
*If you are able and willing to give, may your donation provide*
*abundance for the receivers and expanded blessings for you! Ashé!*

46054168R00178

Made in the USA
San Bernardino, CA
03 August 2019